Hodder & Stoughton

D1350568

30130 106817074

Cover photograph ©: National Portrait Gallery – William Wordsworth. Mary Evans
Picture Library – T.S. Elliot; John Keats; William Blake; Edward Thomas; Gerard Manley
Hopkins. Corbis UK Ltd – Robert Frost.
Mind Maps: Philip Chambers
Illustrations: Karen Donnelly

ISBN 0 340 75327 7

First published 1999
Impression number   10 9 8 7 6 5 4 3 2 1
Year   2002 2001 2000 1999

The 'Teach Yourself' name and logo are registered trade marks of
Hodder & Stoughton Ltd.

Typeset by Transet Limited, Coventry, England.
Printed in Great Britain for Hodder & Stoughton Educational, a division of
Hodder Headline Plc, 338 Euston Road, London NW1 3BH by Cox and Wyman Ltd,
Reading, Berks.

CONTENTS

There are five important things you must know about your brain
and memory to revolutionize
the way you study:

- how your memory
  ('recall') works *while* you are learning
- how your memory works *after* you have finished learning
- how to use Mind Maps – a special technique for helping you
  with all aspects of your studies
- how to increase your reading speed
- how to prepare for tests and exams.

*R*ecall *during learning*
– THE NEED FOR BREAKS

When you are studying, your memory
can concentrate, understand and
remember well for between 20 and 45
minutes at a time. Then it needs a break.
If you carry on for longer than this
without a break your memory starts to
break down. If you study for hours non-stop, you will remember
only a small fraction of what you have been trying to learn, and
you will have wasted hours of valuable time.

So, ideally, *study for less than an hour*, then take a five to ten
minute break. During the break listen to music, go for a walk, do
some exercise, or just daydream. (Daydreaming is a necessary
brain-power booster – geniuses do it regularly.) During the break
your brain will be sorting out what it has been learning, and you
will go back to your books with the new information safely
stored and organized in your memory banks. We recommend
breaks at regular intervals as you work through the Literature
Guides. Make sure you take them!

Recall after learning
— THE WAVES OF YOUR MEMORY

What do you think begins to happen to your
memory straight after you have finished learning something?
Does it immediately start forgetting? No! Your brain actually
increases its power and carries on remembering. For a short
time after your study session, your brain integrates the
information, making a more complete picture of everything it
has just learnt. Only then does the rapid decline in memory
begin, and as much as 80 per cent of what you have learnt can
be forgotten in a day.

However, if you catch the top of the wave of your memory,
and briefly review (look back over) what you have been
studying at the correct time, the memory is stamped in far more
strongly, and stays at the crest of the wave for a much longer
time. To maximize your brain's power to remember, take a few
minutes and use a Mind Map to review what you have learnt
at the end of a day. Then review it at the end of a week, again
at the end of a month, and finally a week before your test or
exam. That way you'll ride your memory
wave all the way there – and beyond!

The Mind Map ®
— A PICTURE OF THE WAY YOU THINK

Do you like taking notes? More importantly, do you like having to
go back over and learn them before tests or exams? Most
students I know certainly do not! And how do you take your
notes? Most people take notes on lined paper, using blue or
black ink. The result, visually, is boring! And what does *your*
brain do when it is bored? It turns off, tunes out, and goes to
sleep! Add a dash of colour, rhythm, imagination, and the whole
note-taking process becomes much more fun, uses more of your
brain's abilities, and improves your recall and understanding.

A Mind Map mirrors the way your brain works. It can be used
for note-taking from books or in class, for reviewing what you
have just studied, and for essay planning for coursework and
in tests or exams. It uses all your memory's natural techniques
to build up your rapidly growing 'memory muscle'.

You will find Mind Maps throughout this book. Study them, add some colour, personalize them, and then have a go at drawing your own – you'll remember them far better! Stick them in your files and on your walls for a quick-and-easy review of the topic.

HOW TO DRAW A MIND MAP

1 Start in the middle of the page. This gives your brain the maximum room for its thoughts.
2 Always start by drawing a small picture or symbol. Why? Because a picture is worth a thousand words to your brain. And try to use at least three colours, as colour helps your memory even more.
3 Let your thoughts flow, and write or draw your ideas on coloured branching lines connected to your central image. These key symbols and words are the headings for your topic. Start like the Mind Map on page xii.
4 Then add facts and ideas by drawing more, smaller, branches on to the appropriate main branches, just like a tree.
5 Always print your word clearly on its line. Use only one word per line.
6 To link ideas and thoughts on different branches, use arrows, colours, underlining, and boxes.

HOW TO READ A MIND MAP

1 Begin in the centre, the focus of your topic.
2 The words/images attached to the centre are like chapter headings, read them next.
3 Always read out from the centre, in every direction (even on the left-hand side, where you will have to read from right to left, instead of the usual left to right).

USING MIND MAPS

Mind Maps are a versatile tool – use them for taking notes in class or from books, for solving problems, for brainstorming with friends, and for reviewing and working for tests or exams – their uses are endless! You will find them invaluable for planning essays for coursework and exams. Number your main branches in the order in which you want to use them and off you go – the main headings for your essay are done and all your ideas are logically organized!

Super speed reading

It seems incredible, but it's been proved – the faster you read, the more you understand and remember! So here are some tips to help you to practise reading faster – you'll cover the ground more quickly, remember more, and have more time left for both work and play.

◆ First read the whole text (whether it's a lengthy book or an exam or test paper) very quickly, to give your brain an overall idea of what's ahead and get it working. (It's like sending out a scout to look at the territory you have to cover – it's much easier when you know what to expect!) Then read the text again for more detailed information.
◆ Have the text a reasonable distance away from your eyes. In this way your eye/brain system will be able to see more at a glance, and will naturally begin to read faster.
◆ Take in groups of words at a time. Rather than reading 'slowly and carefully' read faster, more enthusiastically.
◆ Take in phrases rather than single words while you read.
◆ Use a guide. Your eyes are designed to follow movement, so a thin pencil underneath the lines you are reading, moved smoothly along, will 'pull' your eyes to faster speeds.

Preparing for tests and exams

◆ Review your work systematically. Cram at the start of your course, not the end, and avoid 'exam panic'!
◆ Use Mind Maps throughout your course, and build a Master Mind Map for each subject – a giant Mind Map that summarizes everything you know about the subject.
◆ Use memory techniques such as mnemonics (verses or systems for remembering things like dates and events).
◆ Get together with one or two friends to study, compare Mind Maps, and discuss topics.

AND FINALLY...

Have *fun* while you learn – it has been shown that students who make their studies enjoyable understand and remember everything better and get the highest grades. I wish you and your brain every success! —(Tony Buzan)

HOW TO USE THIS GUIDE

This guide assumes that you have already read at least a few poems from the anthology, although you could read 'How to study a poem' and 'Background' before that. It is best to use the guide alongside the poems.

The 'Commentaries' section can be used in a number of ways. One way is to read a poem and then read the commentary on it, referring to the poem. Then read the poem again to see how it has changed for you, and how well you now understand it. When you come to a test section, test yourself – then have a break!

'Topics for discussion and brainstorming' gives topics that could well feature in exams or provide the basis for coursework. It would be particularly useful for you to discuss them with friends, or brainstorm them using Mind Map techniques (see p. v).

'How to get an "A" in English Literature' gives valuable advice on what to look for in a text, and what skills you need to develop in order to achieve your personal best. 'The exam essay' is a 'night before' reminder of how to tackle exam questions. 'Model answer' gives an example A-grade essay and the Mind Map and plan used to write it.

The questions

Whenever you come across a question in the guide with a star ✪ in front of it, think about it for a moment. You could even jot down a few words in rough to focus your mind. There is not usually a 'right' answer to these questions: it is important for you to develop your own opinions if you want to get an 'A'. The 'Test yourself' sections are designed to take you 10–20 minutes each – which will be time well spent. Take a short break after each one.

TERMS USED

In the Commentaries you will frequently come across the word **stanza**. It simply means any group of one or more lines that is separated by space from any other groups of lines.

Some linked groups of lines also have special names: **couplet** (two lines); **tercet** or **triplet** (three lines); **quatrain** (four lines); **quintet** (five lines); **sextet** or **sixain** (six lines); **sestet** (six lines) – only used in relation to the sonnet, see Glossary; **septet** (seven lines); **octet** (eight lines); **octave** (eight lines); – only used in relation to the sonnet, see Glossary; **decastlich** or **dizain** (ten lines). The **quatrain** is the most common stanza type in European poetry.

EY TO ICONS

Themes

Throughout the commentaries you will find that the themes of religion and nature, and comments on language and poetic technique, are marked by icons. This means that you can find these just by flicking through the book. Go on – try it now!

Religion

Natural world

External Influence

Language

Poetic technique

HOW TO STUDY A POEM

Don't expect to understand a poem after one reading. There are a number of things to look for in a poem:

1 Content: what is it about? The title should help.
2 Is there a specific mood, for example, sad or joyful?
3 Technique: for example, does it rhyme? Are the lines in groups?
4 Rhythm: read the poem aloud, or 'aloud in your head' and listen out for a specific rhythm. This may give you a clue to the poem's mood.
5 Diction: this means the particular vocabulary used for the subject – the poet's choice of words.
6 Punctuation: are the sentences long or short? Does the sense flow from one line to the next, or are there punctuation marks that make you stop?
7 External influences: when was it written? Does it refer to historical events?
8 What facts do you know about the poet's life that may be significant in the poem?

When you have read through the poem again looking our for the above points make a Mind Map of it. The Mind Map on p. xii is a general one for any poem. Now choose a poem from the anthology and make a Mind Map of your own. Using different colours will help you to organize your ideas and remember them later.

When you have completed your Mind Map, read the poem again.

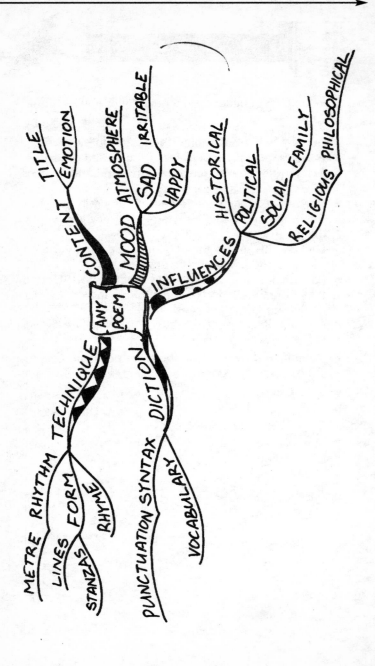

The seven poets span a period of roughly 250 years, and there have been huge historical, religious and social changes during this time. For example Blake, Wordsworth and Keats were born before the British abolished slavery. When William Blake was a teenager, much of North America was still a British colony. Although we might think of T. S. Eliot and Robert Frost as modern writers, both were born before the first car and long before the first aeroplane flew.

There were tremendous social changes in Britain caused by the Industrial Revolution in the latter part of the eighteenth century as people left the countryside to find work in the factories of the towns and cities. These workers were often ruthlessly exploited by the factory owners and the poor conditions eventually led to reforms, the growth of trades unions and the formation of the Labour Party. William Blake's poetry often highlights the poverty endured by London's poor.

During the last years of the eighteenth century, Europe was in turmoil due to the French Revolution and the wars with Napoleon, whilst on the other side of the Atlantic Britain lost its North American colonies. These revolutionary movements in France and North America had a profound influence on intellectual thought. Poets, artists and philosophers discussed the concept of freedom and started to demand social changes. Wordsworth, Keats and others stressed the importance of the individual and the world of the imagination.

With the publication in 1859 of Charles Darwin's book *On the Origin of Species* people started to ask serious questions about Christianity that slowly led to the loosening of the Church's hold on the population. During the early part of the twentieth century the writings and theories of Sigmund Freud (1856–1939) and other psychoanalysts led to a further break with orthodox views of humankind and its place within the universe. Poets like T. S. Eliot explored the apparent meaninglessness of modern life in the light of this new knowledge.

Poetry is important because at its heart is a questioning intelligence and an emotional concern. Blake's compassion for London's poor is still relevant. Concern for the countryside, as expressed by Wordsworth, is something that still interests our media today. Poetry is more than just a communication with the past. The best poems still have something to tell us and they tell it in an unique way that usually makes us feel deeply about the content.

LANGUAGE

Because this anthology spans roughly 250 years there will be words that have changed their meaning since being used in a poem. For example William Blake uses the word *gorge* meaning throat. You may not know this straight away, but the rest of the sentence will tell you that it does not mean a narrow opening between hills – the more familiar modern meaning.

It is important that you look up in a dictionary those words about which you are unsure. One aspect of poetry is its precision of language: the poet will have chosen the exact word. We may talk about 'the woods' in everyday conversation but a poet will use a specific word for a group of trees, such as coppice, copse, forest, grove, hanger or spinney, because each has a precise meaning that will help to convey mood and information. Similarly adjectives, although descriptively accurate, will often be unconventional, adding additional layers of meaning or information. For example Keats's *palaces imperial* (in 'Lamia') suggests that the palaces are in an empire, as well giving a feel for their grandness.

William Wordsworth

Wordsworth (1770–1850) was born in Cumbria and educated at St John's College, Cambridge. In 1790, inspired by the dramatic events of the French Revolution, he went on a walking tour of France and Italy. Late in 1791 he returned to France for a year. This time he fell in love with a young French woman, Annette Vallon, who bore him a daughter. They never married. These events are dealt with in his poems 'Julia', 'Vaudracour' and in the ninth book of 'The Prelude'.

As a young man Wordsworth believed passionately in the French Revolution, republican ideas and individual freedom, so he was deeply disillusioned by the onset of the Terror in France. In 1802 he wrote a sonnet 'To Toussaint l'Ouverture', who had resisted the reintroduction of slavery on Haiti and had been imprisoned.

In 1795 Wordsworth's friend Raisley Calvert left him a legacy enabling him to live as a poet. The early part of his career was spent in the south-west of England where he was close to his friend and fellow poet Samuel Taylor Coleridge. In 1798 they published *Lyrical Ballads*, which is considered to be a landmark of English Romantic poetry. Although this period in Somerset was one of intense creativity for both poets, Wordsworth is usually thought of as the poet of the Lake District, where he moved with his sister in 1799. He married Mary Hutchinson, a school friend, in 1802 and had five children.

In 1813 he was appointed Stamp Distributor for Westmoreland, a position that brought him a comfortable income. He moved to Rydal Mount, Ambleside, where he lived for the rest of his life. The major creative work of his early and middle years was now over and he settled down quietly to being a somewhat conservative and patriotic public man of letters, forgetting the radical ideas of his youth. The final honour of Poet Laureate was bestowed on him in 1843.

The following poems are from his most creative years.

'The Solitary Reaper'

This poem is actually based on a sentence taken from the manuscript of *Tours to the British Mountains*, which was written by Wordsworth's friend Thomas Wilkinson and published much later in 1824. Wordsworth considered the sentence to be particularly fine and adapted it for his poem. The poem follows precisely Wilkinson's observation of the girl, with Wilkinson's final phrase becoming Wordsworth's last line. A girl is observed cutting and then binding the grain. As she does she sings a melancholy song that Wordsworth finds sweeter than either the cuckoo's or the nightingale's. Although he hears her tune he cannot understand the words and wonders whether she is singing of some historic battle or a more mundane song about loss.

Note how the central question (*Will no one tell me what she sings?*) helps to draw the reader into the poem.
❍ Why is it that he cannot understand the words?

Although this is a poem composed from the imagination, Wordsworth gives the illusion of a real event. ❍ How does he do this?

from 'The Prelude' (I)

'The Prelude' is Wordsworth's longest poem, and is usually considered to be his finest achievement. This extract is taken from the middle of the first book. Wordsworth started the poem in 1798, but it was not published until after his death. It is semi-autobiographical and is subtitled 'Growth of a Poet's Mind'. Book I deals with his childhood.

This short extract describes Wordsworth borrowing a boat and rowing out on to the lake. He feels guilty about this as it is not his property (*It was an act of stealth/ And troubled pleasure*). He determines to set a straight course by rowing for a fixed point on the horizon and for a few moments is proud of his achievement as he watches the silvery circles made by the oars in the water. ❍ Look for a **simile** (an image comparing two things) that describes the boat. Suddenly he becomes aware of a brooding presence as a huge peak appears to tower up, blocking out the stars. Although this shape is only a part of the surrounding hills, to the young boy it looks like a baleful giant. Wordsworth is frightened, turns his *bark* (boat) around, and heads back to the shore. Although he tries to rationalize, and realizes the shape that frightened him was not really there, the experience causes him to have bad dreams.

In the first line *her* refers to Nature itself, so Wordsworth is already giving nature a personality. He reinforces this by using words like *head*, *stature*, *strode* to suggest a living being. This technique is called **personification.** ✪ At what time of day does the event take place? Which lines tell you this?

from '**T**he Prelude' (II)

This extract is also from Book I In contrast with the previous extract it recalls the exhilaration of skating on the lake with friends; but as in the previous section Wordsworth slowly moves from the real world into the realm of his imagination, although here it is not a frightening experience. Just as in the previous extract the change in atmosphere takes place as daylight fades. Wordsworth hears the village clock strike 6 o'clock, but continues to skate. He compares himself with an *untired horse* and reinforces this idea with *shod with steel* as both a horse's shoes and the poet's skates would be made of steel. The children make a great deal of noise, which Wordsworth compares with the hunt, with its horn and hounds. Their high-pitched cries are described as being like those of a hunted hare. It gets colder and darker but still they continue to skate until Worsdworth enters an almost trance-like state, when after spinning around he suddenly stops and has the impression of the surrounding hills spinning around him. ❍ Which phrase explains how a skater stops?

As in the first extract it is the natural world that impinges on the poet's senses. Although skating with friends and joining in with their games, the poem also shows that at times he is alone and in tune with his surroundings. ❍ At times Wordsworth really does break away from the games. Which lines tell us this?

'The World is Too much With Us'

This **sonnet** (see Glossary) is in tune with the Romantic movement of its time, in that it regrets the fact that people have lost touch with nature. It says that town dwellers no longer have any affinity with the sea or wind (*Little we see in Nature that is ours*). ❍ Where do you think Wordsworth is standing as he speaks these lines? Do you think that town dwellers are still out of touch with nature?

In the octave (the first eight lines) Wordsworth says that although materialism may have given us many benefits, its distractions mean that we have sacrificed part of our humanity (*We have given our hearts away*). We can no longer get pleasure from watching the raging sea.

In the sestet (the next six lines) Wordsworth declares that he would rather be a pagan than lose such pleasures. For although pagans may be followers of a *creed outworn* and not have the benefits of modern thought, they are more attuned to nature than Wordsworth and his contemporaries. The pagan gods were part of the natural world and were believed to control its elements. Proteus and Triton, characters from classical mythology, are mentioned because both lived in the sea. Proteus could change his shape like the sea, and Triton was the son of the sea god Poseidon. Wordsworth suggests that we have lost part of our humanity by no longer being able to feel nature's power. ✪ Do you think this is true?

Look carefully at the number of lines in this poem and note where the first section ends. ✪ How is it indicated? What else changes at this point?

'To a Skylark'

In the first stanza Wordsworth admires the skylark both for its talent to fly high above the ground and for its cunning ability to drop back to its nest. When the skylark is almost out of sight singing on high, Wordsworth asks whether it is still aware of its earthbound, static nest (*are heart and eye/ Both with thy nest upon the dewy ground*).

In the second stanza the skylark is praised for singing whilst flying high, unlike the nightingale trapped in the wood. Here the skylark is used as a **symbol** (an object representing an idea) for the human spirit's capacity to rise above earthly cares. The last two lines point out that the high and low points of the skylark's soaring flight can be compared with heaven (the sky) and home (the nest). ✪ Why is the skylark compared with a pilgrim in the first line?

'Nutting'

This unrhymed poem about childhood reminds us stylistically of 'The Prelude'. In fact it was originally intended to be a part of that poem. It was written in 1798 when Wordsworth was in Germany and is a reminiscence rather than a description of actual events. Wordsworth tells us elsewhere in a biographical note that as a child he would look for nuts in a wood in the Vale of Esthwaite.

The first sentence shows Wordsworth setting out on his search for hazelnuts. He describes the way he is dressed and what he is carrying. ✪ What do you think he means by *wallet* and *nutting-crook*? How is he dressed? Try drawing him.

Wordsworth then describes his search, how he has pushed through *tangled thickets* and *brambles* until he reaches an

untouched hazel grove. He is delighted by this discovery.
✪ Why is he pleased that there are no broken boughs in the
grove? It has been a struggle to get to this place, so when he
realizes that no one else has found it, he sits down and lets his
imagination roam. Just as in the extracts from 'The Prelude' he
lets nature flood over him as he drifts into a gentle reverie.
After resting he sets about gathering a large harvest of nuts. In
haste he breaks branches, causing damage to the beautiful
grove. He injures so many boughs that he can now see the
intruding sky. Although delighted by his haul of nuts he feels
guilty about the harm he has caused. Remember he was
astonished that there was no damage to the grove when he
arrived. ✪ What is the murmuring sound he hears?
Wordsworth uses this simple tale to show us the importance of
the natural world and that we should respect it.

If you read the poem carefully you will notice that it
appears to fall into several sections, even though there
are no stanzas. As we have seen, the first section describes
him setting out and the clothes that he is wearing. ✪ There are
three more distinct sections. Find them.

'Composed upon Westminster Bridge'

This sonnet is one of Wordsworth's best-known poems.
Wordsworth was not a lover of cities, as in his days they were
particularly dirty, smoke-choked places. All heating and
cooking were done by burning coal or wood – there was no
gas or electricity. You can imagine how cities would have
looked and smelled. Note the simile *like a garment wears*.
However, because it is early in the morning the chimneys are
not yet belching out smoke and the rising sun gives the city a
radiance that reminds Wordsworth of the countryside. In fact
he suggests that for this brief moment the city outshines the
country: *Never did sun more beautifully steep/ In his first
splendour, valley rock or hill*. The use of 'steep' here is
deliberate as it refers to falconry: a hawk's dive on to its prey is
known as a 'stoop'. Wordsworth is reinforcing the comparison
with the countryside ✪ What are the domes and what does he
mean by *temples*?

The 'Lucy' poems

We do not know whether there was a real Lucy. One critic has suggested that she was Welsh, others that she is imaginary but based on Wordsworth's sister Dorothy. However, her identity is unimportant as the poems are about the emotions of longing and loss after her death. Nor is anyone sure whether the poems should be seen as a sequence, or even as one poem. For example 'I Travelled among Unknown Men' was composed several years after the others. Wordsworth does not help us, as he printed the poems in two different arrangements. Three poems are printed here. The usual grouping includes two more.

'I Travelled among Unknown Men'

The poet is travelling abroad and thinks about England and Lucy. He realizes that he loves both his country and the girl he has left. ❂ What is meant by *the wheel* in the third stanza?

'She Dwelt among the Untrodden Ways'

Because of Lucy's isolation her death was known to only a few and these apparently did not care. This is contrasted with the shattering effect her death had on the poet: *The difference to me!* There is something unreal about the girl here, as if she might be a water nymph living beside the River Dove. ❂ What do you think *untrodden* means?

'A Slumber did My Spirit Steal'

As above, the Lucy of this poem seems more of a spiritual being than a real girl. Although the poet is saddened by her death, he takes some solace in the belief that she has become a part of the natural world. ❂ What does *diurnal* mean? If you do not know, try to guess the meaning from the context, then check in a dictionary.

These poems express powerful emotions in the simplest of language. Although the words are relatively easy to understand, Wordsworth seems to have charged them with something stronger than their plain meaning. For example, *unknown men* might just mean foreigners, or it could mean that Wordsworth did not know these men and thus felt alone.

The ambiguity here gives the poems an unreal quality. When he mentions the springs of the River Dove the uncertainty remains, as there are three rivers of that name in England.

Revision points

Wordsworth is usually considered to be a nature poet particularly associated with the Lake District. Whilst much of his poetry is about the natural world, nature is often idealized rather than being portrayed realistically. The purity that he finds in the countryside owes more to his imagination than to reality. Nature is the trigger that sets Wordsworth thinking about the world. As we have seen, 'Nutting' was written long after the events that it portrays. The core of 'Nutting' is in lines 24–43, which present the poet's thoughts as he sits dreaming in the grove. This happens in many of the poems. A description of something, London from Westminster Bridge for example, sets Wordsworth thinking, and the poem records his thoughts. Despite this intellectualism, Wordsworth was deeply moved by nature, finding in the countryside something inspiring, healing and calming.

Much of his poetry deals with the individual. This may be Wordsworth himself in a poem like 'Nutting' or the girl in 'The Solitary Reaper'. In poems where others are involved, such as in the skating episode from 'The Prelude', there are moments when the poet mentions his separateness from the others.

It may not seem so today but Wordsworth deliberately chose to write in a simple way. Previously poetry had used an artificial language that was difficult to understand. It was filled with **allusions** (references) to classical mythology, so that only the well-educated could follow it. Its syntax (the way that its sentences are constructed) was deliberately archaic. Wordsworth's poems are straightforward and read more like stories. 'Nutting' for example, tells a simple tale that is easy to understand.

A Mind Map is an excellent way to remember what has happened in a poem. Here is one for 'The Prelude (1)'. You might want to make your own for other poems.

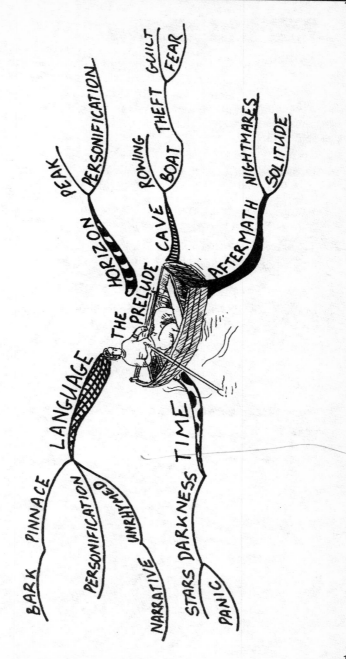

Activities and brain workers

? Without referring to the anthology, write down the titles of the poems from which the following couplets are taken, using the boxes. Try to recall the context of each and how it relates to the rest of the poem.

Nor, England! Did I know till then
  What love I bore to thee.

Dear God! the very houses seem asleep
  And all that mighty heart is lying still!

And growing still in stature the grim shape
  Towered up between me and the stars, and still,

Have sight of Proteus rising from the sea;
  Or hear old Triton blow his wreathèd horn.

Now check your answers. Were they right?

? In the extracts from 'The Prelude' Wordsworth describes two of his boyhood activities. In which other poem does he tells us what he did as a boy? Write down the title.

now you've read the commentary and the Revision Points, take a break before moving on

William Blake

Blake (1757–1827) was the third of seven children born to a London hosier. He did not attend school, but was apprenticed to an engraver at 14. Although he had no formal education, he read widely, accumulating an unorthodox knowledge of religion, history, politics and philosophy. He is seen not only as an important painter, engraver and poet, but also as a mystical visionary and radical thinker, who resisted the orthodoxy of his period and looked for alternatives to the growing and enslaving materialism.

He was a passionate believer in individual freedom and was at odds with conventional religion and politics. In 1803 he was actually charged with high treason for 'uttering seditious and treasonable expressions', but was acquitted. His vivid imagination allowed him to see visions. He believed that he saw and spoke with angels and other biblical figures. This mystical vision of the world and his enthusiasm for freedom have had a wide influence on radical thinking. Blake was an inspiration to many later poets including Allen Ginsberg and the American Beat poets, and the English poet Adrian Mitchell. He has also inspired artists, philosophers, and even scientists.

Although he worked as an engraver, he and his wife Catherine Boucher lived in fairly poor circumstances. Their marriage, though childless, appears to have been a happy one, as they were inseparable. Apart from a brief period in Sussex the Blakes lived in London.

Always in conflict with convention, Blake invented his own method of publishing, illustrating his later work with a complex system that he called 'Illuminated Printing'. This involved engraving the poems backwards onto a copper plate and adding an illustration. After being printed, each page was then hand-coloured. This laborious and difficult process was unique to Blake. The originals are now highly prized. He used this system for a series of long mystical poems usually called the 'Prophetic Books'.

Blake lived through a turbulent period of history that included the American Revolution, the French

Revolution, of which he was a spirited supporter, the first slave revolt in Haiti, led by Toussaint L'Ouverture, and the Napoleonic wars. In England the Industrial Revolution continued to draw people from the countryside to the towns and cities. This social upheaval influenced Blake's view of the world. He was fearful of the growing power of industrialists and the lure of urban living.

During his lifetime and for a quite a long period afterwards, critics thought that Blake's work was either childlike or meaningless. Some, on account of his visions, even thought that he was mad. Now he is recognized as a genius.

'On Another's Sorrow'

In spite of his unorthodox religious views Blake is a Christian believing in a personal God. The poem shows that parents cannot ignore their child's pain. Blake equates this to the Christian God acting as a father to mankind. Blake often uses an everyday example, such as a mother responding to her baby's cry, to examine more complex problems. Here he suggests that if we believe that God created us, then he will respond to our pain in the same way as a mother to her child's.

Note how Blake uses questions and answers to make his points. This is a device he uses in several of his poems. He also uses repetition, as in the third and fourth lines of the third stanza. ✪ Where else in this poem does he do this?

The first part of the poem deals with the parents and child and the last part with how Blake believes God, as a father, looks upon us. ✪ In the middle he introduces the wren. Why do you think he does this?

'The Divine Image'

Although the language is simple – you probably know the actual meaning of every word – it is still difficult to understand exactly what Blake means here. In the first stanza he states that we pray to Mercy, Pity, Peace and Love as they are aspects that make up one idea of God. In the second and third stanzas he tells us that these same qualities could just as easily refer to mankind. ✪ Does this mean that when we pray to God, we are praying to ourselves?

In the last two stanzas he writes that where there is Mercy, Love and Pity there is God. This was a radical idea in Blake's day. Equally revolutionary is the assertion that there is no difference between the races: *all must love the human form/ In heathen, Turk or Jew.* (By *Turk* he means Muslims.) Remember that slavery still existed during Blake's lifetime. Blake is saying that God is not just a god for Christians, as His compassion covers all people irrespective of religion, race or colour. ✪ How do you think his contemporaries would have viewed such an idea? What do you think of his views?

'A *Divine Image*'

On the surface this appears to be the opposite of the previous poem, but in fact Blake proposes that the negative qualities of Cruelty, Jealousy, Terror and Secrecy that are part of man's make up must also be a part of the Creator's, as man was made in God's image. Note the use of personification in the first stanza and its opposite in the second, in which mankind is compared to a forge.

As in the previous poem, the language is simple, with only *gorge* causing difficulty. It means 'throat', and yet it is hard to pin down exactly what he means in using it here. The images in the second stanza are industrial, and will turn up again in his poem 'The Tiger'. ✪ Why do you think Blake uses them?

'*The Tiger*'

Again, like much of Blake's poetry, the meaning is not obvious and yet the individual words are easy enough to understand. As in the previous two poems Blake confronts us with opposites: the terrible nature of the tiger and the meekness of the lamb. He proposes that these opposites are both necessary parts of God's creation. The poem suggests that we cannot fully comprehend a god who is capable of creating such diverse animals.

charmed rept words —

The rhythm is like an incantation, so that the poem *magical* makes its impression by the atmosphere that is created. *effect* The actual meaning of the words is almost secondary. Blake asks a series of questions that have no answers, yet they instil

15

a sense of wonder and even fear. Many of the phrases are deliberately ambiguous, forcing the reader to search for possible meanings. Even a simple phrase like *burning bright* could be interpreted in a variety of ways. It could just refer to the tiger's dramatic colouring, or to its eyes shining *In the forests of the night*, or perhaps to the tiger's ferocity, or its burning passion. It is also worth remembering that Blake would have used acid in his work as an engraver, and so he may be remembering how that burns.

This was written at a time of growing industrialization and Blake uses the images of the factory and workshop to explain the power of a creator. The tiger is obviously made of flesh and bone yet the imagery is of metal and fire.

Read the first and last stanzas again. They are almost the same.
✪ What is the difference and why do you think Blake made it?

'The Clod and the Pebble'

The first and last stanzas offer two contrasting interpretations of love. The first is sung by the soft clod of clay and the second by the hard unyielding pebble. The clod says that love is about giving to others, whereas the hard pebble thinks of love in selfish terms. Blake does not comment on these opposing ideas. ✪ Which stanza do you think gives the better depiction of love?

Note how Blake uses the same rhyme scheme in the first and last stanzas. Use letters to mark the rhymes. ✪ How is the rhyme scheme different in the second stanza? Why do you think Blake uses rhyme in this way?

'Holy Thursday'

This title refers to the annual service of Thanksgiving at St Paul's Cathedral, London. Holy Thursday is Maundy Thursday, it commemorates Christ washing the disciples' feet. It was a time of celebration and giving in London's great church; but all that Blake sees is the demeaning poverty of London's children. This is a powerful political poem as it condemns the hypocrisy surrounding a major religious occasion. As in other poems Blake poses contrasting points. He says that in a land where the *sun does shine/ And where'er the rain does fall* – by which he means England – there should be enough food for everyone. He wonders why in reality *It is a land of poverty* for so many. Once again he uses questions to make the reader consider what is happening. ✪ What does *usurous* mean? Look it up if you do not know. Who is making the *trembling cry*?

'The Garden of Love'

The Garden of Love represents innocence and freedom, quite possibly sexual freedom. However, since Blake's last visit to the garden a chapel has been built where he used to play. The chapel represents organized religion, which Blake detested. He felt that it deliberately constrained the individual's freedom with its *'Thou shalt not'* attitude. Blake believed that the joy of religious life was curbed by the black-gowned priests. This is a deliberate attack on the Church and a daring thing to write in Blake's time. ❂ Why are the gates of this chapel shut?

As in much of Blake's work the *Garden* and the *Chapel* are not real, but symbols for freedom and repression. Symbols are often used in poetry. ❂ Can you think of other ways in which the symbol of a garden has been used to denote freedom or innocence?

'Infant Sorrow'

On the surface this is a poem about childbirth, but there is an underlying religious element. The child soon discovers that it cannot struggle for long in its father's hands and that it is easier to acquiesce, *To sulk upon my mother's breast*. A new born child is weak and dependent on its mother and yet it apparently leapt into the world ready for a struggle. We can attempt psychological interpretations. For example, the child may be rebelling against its father. Note the restraint of the swaddling bands. ❂ What has wearied the baby?

'He Who Bends ...'

This quatrain states quite clearly that if you chase after something too strongly you will destroy it, and that it is far better to accept, to go with the flow in order to obtain your desires or needs. ❂ How far do you agree with Blake?

'London'

This is a savage indictment on the poverty and deprivation that Blake observed during his walks through the city. He speaks of the *mind-forg'd manacles*, of conventional ideas, organized religion, and the political system, that grind down the poor and keep them in their place. This is a powerful attack on the way the country is ruled. There are two words here that you may not have come across before. *Charter'd* means by Royal Charter, thus suggesting privilege; and perhaps restriction. *Manacles* is another word for fetters or chains.

Blake mentions two 'professions' that have always been available to the poor. Men could become soldiers, and die or be maimed defending the system: *And the hapless soldier's sigh/ Runs in blood down palace walls.* Women could become prostitutes. There were around 50,000 prostitutes working in London at this time. As Blake walked through the city he would have seen soldiers and prostitutes, and no doubt felt sorry for them both.

Note how words often work on more than one level. For example *black'ning church* might describe the dirty façade, the soot-covered brickwork, especially as Blake mentions the *chimney-sweeper* in the previous line. It might refer back to the black-gowned priests in 'The Garden of Love' or alternatively suggest that the Church is a darkening and restrictive force.

Like 'The Tiger' this poem has an obvious rhythm, which is reinforced by repetitions, for example of *every*, which hammer home Blake's message. An ABAB rhyme scheme and mainly **masculine rhymes** (see **rhymes** in Glossary) also give strength to the poem. Another of Blake's techniques is to use opposites. One example is marriage and death, seen in *marriage hearse.* Yet weddings should be happy events and funerals melancholy. The Church was involved with both ceremonies and we already know what Blake thought about organized religion. ✪ Do you think that Blake is in favour of marriage? Why should he couple marriage to the hearse?

'Never Seek to Tell thy Love'

This poem implies more than it actually says. Blake intimates that it is difficult to understand what love is and that if one tries too hard then one can lose love altogether. Blake may very well be saying that mortals cannot understand love and that we should just accept it when it happens. The first stanza states this, but in the next two the speaker admits his devotion to his love and then loses her, perhaps to a passing traveller. ✪ Why do you think the loved one leaves? Who or what is the traveller?

from 'Auguries of Innocence'

This is an extract from a much longer poem. It opens with a catalogue of abuses against animals. During this period there were no societies for the prevention of cruelty to animals, and

19

animals were treated abominably. Bull-baiting, bear pits and cock-fighting were normal pursuits; songbirds were blinded and kept in cages. It was believed that they would sing better if they were blind (*a robin redbreast in a cage*).

In the opening quatrain, which is sometimes printed separately, Blake suggests that there is a universality to creation and that the destruction of the smallest creature has a diminishing effect. This is the poem's main theme. Having stated this, Blake follows it up with a series of couplets that reinforce the message that wanton cruelty to any of God's creatures is an affront to the natural order. The important thing is that Blake is condemning pointless cruelty. The slaughter of animals for us to eat is justified, *The lamb misus'd breeds public strife,/ And yet forgives the butcher's knife*. It is the same for carnivores like the wolf and lion who can kill prey for food. This is not cruelty, but nature.

Today we are familiar with the atom and the vast expanse of the cosmos. Photographs have given us an idea of what they are like. Blake was aware of them too, even though such scientific knowledge was not yet available. Visionaries like Blake can make these leaps and can imagine that a grain of sand could contain a whole world.

Blake writes that *A horse misus'd upon the road/ Calls to Heaven for human blood.* ✪ Do you agree with this? Why is it cruel to keep doves and pigeons in a dove-house? Look how each couplet is rhymed and note how many of the rhymes are strong masculine ones, rhyming on the final stressed syllable of a line.

There are several words here that now need some explanation: *Augury* means prophecy; a *Cherubim* is a type of angel; a *Game-cock* is a fighting cock; and a *Chafer* is a type of beetle.

'A *Poison Tree*'

Here Blake points out that if one is honest about anger (*wrath*), then it will not harm you. However, if it is repressed it will grow stronger. This is shown in the first stanza: *I told my wrath, my wrath did end*, and *I told it not, my wrath did grow*. As in other poems Blake puts forward his belief that strong emotions are part of human nature, and are only dangerous when denied. The poem goes on to show what happens when anger is allowed to build up and fester. The final stanza is **ironic** (see Glossary): Blake is not really glad at his foe's discomfort. This is his way of showing that he has been diminished by his own heartlessness.

❂ Why does Blake compare the growing emotion to an apple tree? Can you think of other stories where an apple has significance?

Revision points

Although he despised organized religion Blake was a committed Christian and evolved his own system of belief that stressed the importance of the individual. He was also keenly aware of the terrible poverty that he saw in London and of the exploitation of workers. These concepts underpin much of his poetry. A poem like 'The Garden of Love' attacks the Church, and 'Holy Thursday' and 'London' are political assaults on the way the country was ruled.

His visionary experiences, which were not drug nor alcohol induced, gave him many psychological insights long before the world was aware of the workings of the unconscious

Blake's view of the world is complex as it deals with extremes, yet he sees these opposites as part of a universal system. He does not condemn humankind's weaknesses, but rather accepts them as part of our individuality. It is the same when he writes of spiritual matters. God is not just a simple father figure to him, but a personal creator responsible for all aspects of life, good and evil, the tiger and the lamb.

In general Blake uses a plain vocabulary, yet it is often difficult to extract a precise meaning from the poem as a whole. His verse may appear naïve, with its simple rhyme schemes and end-rhymes, but it is in fact technically accomplished. Poetic devices such as repetition are used to emphasize a point (In *every* cry of *every* Man,/ In *every* Infant's cry of fear); the use of unanswerable questions (*What the hammer? What the chain?*) forces the reader to consider, not only the questions, but their possible answers. These devices, together with a strong musical rhythm and deliberate rhymes, create an atmosphere or mood that conveys more than just what the words mean. Even when we cannot always follow the logic of the words, we still understand something from the poem.

Remember drawing a Mind Map will help you to remember.

Activities and brain workers

?   Think about the poem 'The Tiger'. Read it again noting Blake's use of questions. Now write down your own questions about how you might make a tiger. For example you could ask, 'What paintbrush marked your stripes?' In the space below write down your own questions trying to make them sound like Blake's.

> What paintbrush marked your stripes?

?   Do your questions sound like Blake's? Try writing a stanza like the second one in 'The Tiger' using your own questions.

?   The following four lines are printed in the wrong order. Without looking at the poem, rearrange them so as they make sense. The punctuation may give you a clue.

Doth the wingèd life destroy;
Lives in Eternity's sunrise.
But he who kisses the Joy as it flies
He who bends to himself a joy

Now check and see if you are right.

stop thinking about poetry and visionary experiences — you deserve a break

John Keats

Keats (1795–1821) was the eldest child of a London livery stables manager. His short life was touched with family tragedy as his father died when Keats was eight. His mother remarried and died six years later of tuberculosis. His younger brother Tom died in 1818. At about this time he fell in love with Fanny Brawne and remained in love with her until his own early death from tuberculosis in Rome.

Keats received a reasonable education that would have included lessons in Greek, Latin and French literature. In 1810 he was apprenticed to an apothecary-surgeon, but cancelled his fifth year and enrolled as a student at Guy's Hospital. In 1816 he was granted a licence to practise as an apothecary (pharmaceutical chemist), but he soon gave up medicine in order to devote himself to poetry. His first book was published in 1817. Though there were some favourable reviews, sales were poor. Later that year the book received a harsh review from John Lockhart, who referred to Keats and other young poets as the 'Cockney School of Poetry'. Lockhart had a reputation for savage criticism, hence his nickname 'the Scorpion'. Lockhart attacked Keats's poem 'Endymion' in a condescending manner, advising Keats to return to his 'plasters, pills and ointment boxes'. Hurt as he was by such attacks Keats was sure of his vision as a poet and continued to write.

His writing career was short: he composed nearly all of his poetry in the years 1816–19. His letters, which were published in 1848 and 1878, are now regarded as important. They are written mainly to Fanny Brawne, to his sister and brothers, as well as to friends and fellow poets such as Leigh Hunt and Shelley. Some of the letters contain valuable comments on the poems, whilst others are concerned with everyday events in his life. They have a great delicacy and some lines have become a part of the English language, ... *load every rift of your subject with ore* (letter to Shelley). T. S. Eliot called them 'certainly the most notable and most important ever written by any English poet'.

from 'Isabella'

These two stanzas are taken from a poem of 63 stanzas, the full title of which is 'Isabella, or The Pot of Basil'. Keats borrowed the story from the Italian writer Giovanni Boccacio (1313–75). The poem tells the tale of Isabella and her lover Lorenzo. Lorenzo, a mere clerk, was considered unworthy to marry her by her two brothers, so they killed him and buried him in a wood, telling their sister that Lorenzo had gone abroad. Isabella has a dream in which Lorenzo tells her where he is buried. She finds the body and brings its head home, hiding it in a garden pot full of basil. The brothers discover it and then flee abroad, and as expected in such tales the inconsolable Isabella goes mad.

There was at that time a demand for macabre and gothic stories of this kind. The poem is particularly interesting as it is written in the Italian verse form known as *ottava rima*. *Ottava* means eight. ❂ Look at these stanzas and find out to what the 'eight' refers.

These stanzas deal with the murder. Note how Keats foreshadows this by calling Lorenzo *their murder'd man* when in actual fact he is still riding beside them. ❂ How does Keats describe the brothers' complexions? *Straiten'd* is an old word meaning narrow.

from 'Lamia'

This extract is from a poem of over 700 lines. As in 'Isabella', Keats has reinterpreted a much older story. The 'lamia' of the title is a serpent which has been transformed into a woman by the god Hermes. Lycius, a Corinthian, falls in love with her, and insists on giving a party in her honour despite her protests. An uninvited guest sees through her disguise and when he calls her by name she vanishes. Lycius is grief-stricken and dies. It is a **narrative poem** (one telling a story) appealing to the Romantic taste for unusual and macabre stories.

This extract gives an impression of the bustling city of Corinth. ❂ What time of day do you think it is and why? Although about a busy city of *populous streets*, there is a lethargic tone to the lines. How do you think that has been achieved?

*from '**T**he Eve of St Agnes'*

These three extracts are from another narrative poem. It is set in the mediaeval period, telling the story of Madeline and her lover Porphyro. There is a legend that on St Agnes Eve a girl will dream of her lover if she performs certain rituals. Porphyro, who is disliked by Madeline's father, is smuggled into her bedroom, where he hides. Madeline returns to her bedroom and says her prayers in the hope of dreaming about her lover. While she is asleep Porphyro sings to her, and when she wakes up from her dream to find him at her bedside, she thinks that she is still dreaming. They declare their love for each other. Because Madeline's father would not accept Porphyro as her husband, they decide to flee from the castle in spite of the terrible storm outside.

This is considered by many to be one of Keats' finest poems because of its language and the powerful atmosphere he creates. It is written in a complex verse form known as the Spenserian stanza that requires a great deal of skill particularly with the involved rhyme pattern. It is named after the poet Edmund Spenser (c.1552–99) who invented it for his famous poem 'The Faerie Queene'. ✪ What do you notice about the last line of each stanza?

The first extract describes the night's bitter cold, as a Beadsman (one who counts the beads on his rosary and is employed to say prayers for his master) walks amongst the tombs in the castle chapel. On leaving the chapel he is confronted by the sudden contrast of music and gaiety coming from the castle. ✪ What stops the Beadsman from entering the warmth of the castle?

In the second extract Madeline has returned to her bedroom from the music and festivities. She is eager to dream of her lover. She kneels to pray and the light from the casement, so marvellously described in Stanza XXIV makes her look like an angel. Porphyro who is hiding in the chamber watches her. ✪ What is meant by *Rose-bloom* in Stanza XXV? Where has it come from?

The final section describes Madeline and Porphyro leaving the castle. ✪ How do you know that the storm is still raging? Why doesn't the porter challenge them? Keats creates a vivid picture of the mediaeval castle with its tapestry (*arras*) and its sombre lighting. ❂ There is a good description of the tapestry. How well can you picture it in your mind's eye?

Although you have only three short extracts it is easy to note the way Keats holds his reader's attention with the constant contrasts: warmth/cold, passionate life/world weary death, youth/age, the fully awake lovers/the sleeping castle. It is these opposites that give a magical feel to the castle. The main characters are larger than life, the world-weary Beadsman waiting to die, the innocent Madeline and the daring Porphyro, who has risked all to hide in Madeline's chamber. Keats's descriptions are so intense that a reader has a strong visual sense of how the castle looked. It may just be minor items such as *A Chain-drooped lamp* or the tapestry *rich with horseman, hawk and hound* (note the **alliteration**), but it is this attention to detail that makes the poem memorable. ❂ Why are the lovers able to escape so easily?

Much of the intensity is due to the Spenserarian stanza and its involved rhyme scheme. ❂ Use letters to mark the rhymes and then try to write your own stanza on a castle following the rhyme pattern.

'Ode to Autumn'

The word 'ode' is from the Greek *aeidein*, meaning to sing or chant, and was originally applied to a formal ceremonial poem. Now it means a poem that respectfully praises its subject. Keats wrote a number of odes, of which this is one of the best in the English language.

The theme is obvious with the first stanza celebrating the season's natural abundance. In the second stanza Autumn is personified as a drowsy figure associated with the harvest and is half-glimpsed in a rural setting, *sitting careless on a granary floor*, or *on a half-reap'd furrow sound asleep*. The poem moves from the fertile fullness of the first stanza through the languorous feel of the second, to a melancholic sadness in the third where Spring is remembered. However, this sadness at the season's ending is lightened by the knowledge that Spring will return and that the progression of the seasons is the natural order. ❂ Why do you think that the swallows are gathering? Does the robin (*red-breast*) represent any particular season?

Note the number of words that end in 'ing' that give an extra dimension of rhythm. In the first stanza 'l' and 'm' sounds are dominant, helping to give that overripe feeling to the verse. But it is the stately metre and rhyming that are the poem's true glory, giving the sense of maturity, fullness and completion that Keats associates with autumn.

'Ode to a Nightingale'

The poem appears to be about Keats's thoughts as he hears the nightingale's song; but underlying this there is a meditation on life and death.

STANZA 1

Whilst listening to the nightingale (*thou, light-wingèd Dryad of the trees*) Keats feels as though he is drugged or intoxicated.

This is strengthened by the use of words like *numbness*, *hemlock* (a plant from which a sedative can be extracted), *opiate*, and *Lethe* (the river of forgetfulness). The poet is in a highly excited state, so happy that it is almost painful.

STANZA 2

The poet wishes for an even deeper intoxication associated with wine, sun and the South of France (Provence). Provence has a special place in European Literature as its poets (the troubadours) invented a number of forms that influenced later cultures. These desires are so powerful that the poet contemplates leaving the world and joining the nightingale in the forest. It is these ideas that suggest a Romantic concern with death.

STANZA 3

If it were possible to join the nightingale Keats could leave behind all the pain associated with life. Just below the poem's surface Keats muses on mortality and how everything grows old, loses its beauty and dies (*Where youth grows pale, and spectre-thin, and dies*).

STANZA 4

Here Keats turns away from the intoxication of wine, believing that poetry itself can take him into the enchanted world of the nightingale's song. Bacchus is the god of wine, whose chariot was pulled by leopards (*pards*). Keats rejects his influence insisting that the *viewless wings of poesy* are sufficient. 'Viewless' here means hidden from view, hence invisible.

STANZA 5

Still intoxicated by the nightingale's song he can no longer see the flowers in the gathering darkness and is only aware of their perfume.

STANZA 6

The moment is now so ecstatic that Keats contemplates death as he listens to the song. He cannot conceive of anything being so fulfilling again. In the last two lines he changes his mind. The nightingale would continue to sing over his grave (*sod*), but he would not be alive to hear it.

STANZA 7

Keats states that the nightingale has a kind of immortality, as all through history others, both high-born and peasant, have heard its song and been mesmerized in a similar way (*The voice I hear this passing night was heard/ In ancient days by emperor and clown*).

STANZA 8

Stanza 7 ends with the word *forlorn*, which acts as a device to drag the poet back to the real world. The experience had been so intense that he is unsure whether it was a dream or reality. Note the simile in the first line.

In this poem it is difficult to separate reality from fantasy. The nightingale's song is the trigger that allows Keats to enter a private world and half-believe that he could preserve it for ever by dying (stanza 6).

✪ Is there anything odd about the line lengths? If so, which line is the odd one out?

Revision points

Keats rarely focuses on what most people regard as the real world, his poems being set either in a mythical past or in his dream world. He is more concerned with impressions and the realm of the imagination.

However, in all of the poems and extracts here, there is a tension between this dream world and reality, between the intellectual comfort of the imagination and the often difficult experiences of real life. Keats contemplates death in 'Ode to a Nightingale', but chooses to live. The magical qualities of the autumn harvest give way to the routine changing of the seasons ('Ode to Autumn'). Even in the narrative 'The Eve of St Agnes' Madeline is forced to flee from the castle's safety and brave the terrors of the storm. However powerful the imagination, Keats realizes that the real world of impermanence, change and mortality is always with us – we cannot truly escape it.

The first things one notices about Keats's poems are the sensuousness of the language and the attention to detail. Often he describes things in terms of something else. In the first stanza of 'Ode to a Nightingale' he does not say that he is tired or dreaming, but compares his frame of mind to that of someone who is drugged. Note his unusual word combinations, such as *sunburnt mirth*, which means far more than the words' individual meanings. When writing about alcohol in the second stanza he says that it tastes of Flora, the Roman goddess of flowers and spring. This is more potent than saying the wine tastes of flowers. Then he asks for *a beaker full of the warm South*, meaning the South of France, which has already been alluded to by the mention of *Provençal song*. Provence is a wine growing area of southern France. But he also wants the wine to be full of Hippocrene, a fountain on Mount Helicon in Greece that was sacred to the Muses and thus to poetry. In a few lines Keats has charged words with more than their everyday meanings and piled on layers of allusion (references). There is almost too much to take in at first reading.

Often he only wants to give an impression of states of mind, yet he can also use his descriptive powers to give us almost photographic representations of places, such as the description of the stream in 'Isabella', the intricate detail of the window in Stanza XXIV of the 'Eve of St Agnes', and of the castle itself. It is the intensity of the language that draws us into Keats's poems.

Don't forget, a Mind Map will help you to absorb the descriptive detail in a poem like 'The Eve of St Agnes'.

Activities and brain workers

?   If you had to make a film of 'Isabella', which actors would you cast for the heroine, the murdered Lorenzo and the two villains? Discuss this with friends.

?   The Mind Map overleaf shows the positive elements in Keats's 'Ode to Autumn'. Add to it, or draw one of your own, showing the other things that Keats writes about autumn. Look particularly at the third stanza.

?   'Lamia' is written in rhyming couplets and is mainly a description of the city of Corinth. Try writing a few rhyming couplets about your own city, town or village.

Read stanzas XXIV and XXV of 'The Eve of St Agnes' again and either write your own prose description of the window, or make a drawing.

stop reading and take your eyes for a walk, or make yourself a drink, so as to come back refreshed and ready to study

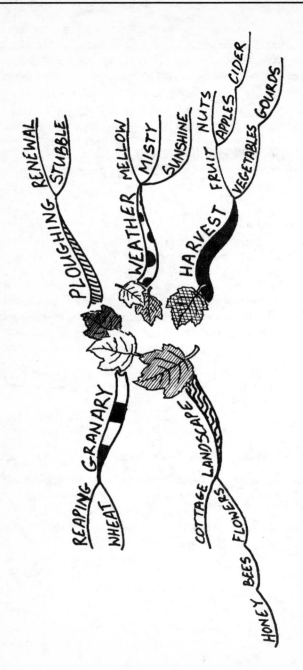

Gerard Manley Hopkins

Hopkins (1844–89) was born in Essex to middle class parents who were strong believers in the Anglican church; they were also interested in the arts. He was educated at Balliol College, Oxford, where he wrote a number of poems, including 'Heaven-Haven'. At Oxford he came under the influence of John Henry Newman, who had converted from Anglicanism to the Roman Catholic Church. Newman was created cardinal in 1879. Hopkins made the same difficult journey, being accepted into the Roman Catholic faith in 1866. Two years later he decided to become a Jesuit priest and symbolically burned all his poems, although he sent some copies to his friend and fellow poet Robert Bridges. He wrote little in the next few years whilst he was a novice at Roehampton. He went on to study at St Beuno's in Wales where, among other things, he learnt Welsh.

During this period he analysed poetic rhythms. This led to his own system called **sprung rhythm** (see Glossary). He based this on the patterns of classical Greek and Latin poetry, plus the formal rhymes of Welsh poetry. Classical poetry is unrhymed and depends rhythmically on a repeated pattern of stressed and unstressed units in each line. Welsh poetry has an involved rhyme structure.

His returned to writing poetry and in 1876 completed his most ambitious poem 'The Wreck of the Deutschland'. It was rejected by the Jesuit journal *The Month* as being too difficult. Following his ordination as a priest he served in several industrial parishes, including Liverpool. He worked as a priest for a short period in Glasgow, where he was appalled by the poverty and vice that he encountered. This short period also made him aware of his own shortcomings as a parish priest. After visiting Loch Lomond he wrote the poem 'Inversnaid'. In 1884 he went to teach Greek and Latin at University College, Dublin, but he found the academic workload intolerable, becoming ill and depressed. In his last few years he wrote only a handful of poems. He died of typhoid.

Hardly any of his poems were published during his lifetime. It was left to Robert Bridges to collect them and publish them in

1918. They were met with bewilderment at first, but they steadily found a readership. Hopkins is now recognized as an important innovator and major poet. His output is small and strongly influenced by his religious beliefs.

'Inversnaid'

The first three stanzas describe a stream (*burn*) descending a hillside. The fourth is a plea for the preservation of such wild wetlands (*O let them be left, wildness and wet*). The poem has an immediate impact because of its rhymes and rhythm. When you read the poem aloud, it is impossible to miss the rhythm.

Hopkins joins words together (*rollrock*) making a new word that means more than just 'roll' and 'rock'. *Fell-frowning* makes a stronger impression than 'frowning like a fell'. ○ Try doing this yourself by combining words so that when they are joined, they express something more than their separate meanings. Other things to watch out for are alliteration and repetition of sounds such as the 'r' sound that runs through the second line of the third stanza. His choice of words is precise, as they all help to produce his distinctive rhythm. The poem is rich with alliteration and internal rhymes. ○ Pick out some rhymes where one of the words is not at the line end; for example, 'let' and 'wet' in the last stanza.

'Heaven-Haven'

An early poem written during Hopkins's student days, this is simpler in structure than 'Inversnaid'. Hopkins has not yet developed his rhythmical system, nor are there any compound words like *rollrock*. However, there are phrases such as *out of the swing of the sea* that appear to be moving towards his later technique.

The subtitle tells you that it is a poem about a nun entering a convent where she will be free of the world's anxieties (*Where no storms come*). She looks forward to a life of calm and freedom from stress. The poem is an extended metaphor. ○ What are havens? Why are they dumb?

'Felix Randall'

This refers to the time when Hopkins, as a parish priest, would visit the sick and dying. In the first four lines he recalls that the blacksmith (*farrier*) was once robust, but now both his physical and mental health have declined. ✪ Which phrase describes his mental deterioration? In the next four lines the poet records that over a period he brought comfort to the man, who was previously unable to come to terms with illness, and helped to reconcile him with God. In lines 9–11 Hopkins explains how the man's decline and death have touched him personally. Hopkins is spiritually enriched through performing this priestly duty. The remaining lines depict the blacksmith in his prime, his *boisterous years*, when he never thought about the possibility of ill health.

The poem is about Felix Randall, but Hopkins is also reminding us of our own mortality. The poem is rich with alliteration. Pick out some examples. ✪ What do you think is meant by the *random grim forge*?

A *farrier* is a special type of blacksmith who works only with horses. *Fettle* is a dialect word meaning to put in order, get ready or mend. We still use the word in the expression 'in fine fettle', meaning in good condition. A *drayhorse* is a heavy horse that pulls a dray, a low flat cart without sides often used by brewers to transport beer barrels. *Sandals* in this context are horseshoes.

'Spring and Fall'

There is a double meaning in the title. In the USA fall means autumn, so the poem's title means Spring and Autumn. To a Roman Catholic *fall* suggests humankind's fall from grace because of Adam's 'original sin', so there is also a religious element.

✝ The doctrine of 'original sin' is an important concept to Roman Catholics. According to their beliefs humankind is born into sin because of Adam's and Eve's first sin in the Garden of Eden. As we are descended from Adam and Eve, we are all burdened with their guilt from birth. All of our sorrow and suffering is due to the recognition of this fact.

🌳 The poem's opening lines deal with the young girl's distress as she watches the falling leaves (*unleaving*). The young girl (Margaret) could be thought of as being in her springtime, so there is an allusion to the title. Hopkins then writes that the falling leaves are like *the things of man* which points to the religious implications. As the girl grows up she will no longer be saddened by the falling leaves, but none the less, because humankind is born into sin, she will still know sorrow. Margaret's sadness and the fall of man are interwoven, as both the leaves and the girl are 'fallen'. Even though Hopkins shows compassion for the child's innocence, he knows that from the religious viewpoint she is as tainted by sin as any other mortal (*It is the blight that man was born for*).

Non-Catholics may find the concept of 'original sin' rather uncompromising; but for a Roman Catholic priest the belief is central.

❷ What do you imagine are her *fresh thoughts*? What do you understand by the word *Goldengrove*? Is it a compound of two words, or an actual place?

'Spring'

This is a sonnet in celebration of spring. The octave (first eight lines) presents a series of images associated with spring. Fresh growth, birds nesting, thrushes' eggs, new leaves, blossom, newborn lambs flash before us like bits of a film. Note the use of the word *blue* to recall the blue of a thrush's egg as well as the blue of spring skies.

The sestet (next six lines) relates Spring's beauty to innocence, particularly to the time before man's fall from grace, when Adam and Eve were innocent in the Garden of Eden. Spring is *A strain of the earth's sweet being in the beginning,* the beginning meaning The Garden of Eden. Hopkins then prays to God to protect childhood innocence *before it cloy* and becomes *sour with sinning.*

The octave is straightforward as we easily respond to the natural world. In the sestet Hopkins ties in Spring's freshness with the innocence of the Garden of Eden. He seems to be asking why Spring, like innocence, must fade.

The rhythm is heightened by a number of rhythmical devices such as alliteration (*When weeds in wheels*), vowel repetitions (*shoot long and, lovely*) and internal rhymes (*lush/thrush*) ✪ Pick out other examples.

'Pied Beauty'

This is an exuberant celebration of all of the pied, dappled, two-coloured things created by God. It is not just about the animals, but also the landscape *plotted and pierced* and the everyday world of work, *all trades, their gear and tackle.*

It is a hymn of praise to God for creating a diversely beautiful world. ✪ Write down any similes you can find and think about what they achieve.

The poem is short and yet Hopkins appears to have crammed in a wide variety of things that express a dappledness. The poem praises a god who can make so many wondrous things part of a single and cohesive creation. ✪ Which words express this pied (two-coloured) quality?

'Binsey Poplars'

The first stanza is a lament for the felled trees. The poem is based on an actual event in the Oxfordshire village of Binsey. ◐ What word does Hopkins use for poplars? Where are the trees sited? The second stanza is also a lament, but here it is for humankind that does not understand what is lost when trees are cut down, or when the earth is dug up (*delve*). Hopkins writes that even when we try to improve things (*To mend her*), we still cause damage because of our ignorance of the wholeness of creation. Once something beautiful has been destroyed, it cannot be replaced and in time is forgotten: *Aftercomers cannot guess the beauty been*. According to Hopkins our insensitivity to nature is due to the fact that we cannot comprehend God's overall plan because of the fall from grace that ensnares us from birth.

There are a number of rhythmical devices at work. There are the end-rhymes; but also internal rhymes like *dandled/ sandalled*, alliteration and repetition. ◐ Write down examples of these. ◐ What is meant by the *sleek and seeing ball*?

'The Starlight Night'

This is another sonnet with the *octave* describing the beauty of the night sky and expressing wonder at God's creation. Hopkins notes that when we stare into the sky, some of us make pictures with the stars suggesting *bright boroughs* and *circle-citadels*. The *fire folk* probably refers to mythology as many groups of stars represent ancient heroes such as the constellation of Orion the hunter. ◐ What are the *flake-doves*? Why do you think they are *floating forth*?

In the sestet Hopkins asks how we can repay God for this glory, and then supplies the answer: *Prayer, patience, alms, vows*. Hopkins then reminds us of the octave by repeating *Look*, the first word of the poem, and returning to the night sky, which is now compared to the spring (*a Mayness, like on orchard boughs*). The allusion to spring is another reminder of lost innocence. The final line recalls that children are often told that Christ, the Virgin Mary and the saints (*his hallows*) live in the heavens or sky. In fact there is something deliberately naïve about the poem. Hopkins assumes a childlike view of the heavens in order to produce a greater sense of wonder. ✪ What are the *shocks*? Do you know other words for them? Where are they?

As in 'Spring' the octave is straightforward, and it is the sestet that carries the more involved religious content.

'In the Valley of the Elwy'

In the first stanza Hopkins remembers the kindness that he received when visiting friends. From the moment that he steps into their house he feels their warmth. He wonders whether their friendliness was influenced by the beauty of where they lived. In the second stanza he praises the landscape and natural beauty of Wales, but points out that the Welsh do not appear to be affected for the better by such beauty. The poem ends with Hopkins asking God to help the Welsh (*the inmate*) to overcome their deficiencies. The point behind this poem is that there should be harmony between humankind and the natural world. As in 'Pied Beauty' Hopkins puts forward the idea that there ought to be a sympathy between humanity and the world created by God. ✪ How many lines are there in the poem? What kind of a poem could it be?

'My Own Heart ...'

This sonnet and the next poem were written towards the end of Hopkins's life when he was ill and depressed. In the octave he prays for release from his suffering, yet realizes that this is unlikely to come. He compares his groping for comfort to a blind man's difficulties, or to a thirsty seaman being tormented by the undrinkable salt water surrounding him. The *world of wet* means the sea. He wonders why it is that he, as a priest, cannot find comfort: *My own heart let me have more pity on*.

In the sestet Hopkins acknowledges that only God will be able to resolve his anguish and that he must have patience and not worry (*call off thoughts awhile*).

The poem deals with a priest's spiritual and psychological crisis (*with this tormented mind tormented yet*). ✪ What is the *lovely mile* of the last line? What do you notice about the word that rhymes with *mile*? *Betweenpie* is a made up word. What could it mean?

'Thou art indeed just, Lord ...'

This is another despairing poem, written in the last year of Hopkins's life, in which he thinks that everything he has done has been of little value. He asks God why sinners should prosper, when he, a priest, appears to be beset by failure. The poem may be related to the loss of his creative powers as well as to the spiritual crisis that he is enduring. Note the plainness of the language and the lack of compound words. Even the rhythm has a heavier feel. The opening four lines, with some minor alterations, are from the Bible (Jeremiah XII). He takes several other ideas from this chapter, so it is a good idea to read it. It will help you to get closer to what Hopkins means in this pessimistic poem.

He looks for solace in the natural world, so often the source of past inspiration. He writes about it briefly, yet it offers no consolation. There is just a ray of hope in the last line when he calls on God to help (*send my roots rain*). ❂ Why do you think that he refers to himself as *Time's eunuch*?

Revision points

For Hopkins everything that exists is an integral part of God's creation. There is nothing haphazard in the natural world. It is all part of some glorious conception. Many of his poems are like hymns.

His poetry looks and sounds different because of the sensuousness of the language and the surprising rhythms. Even the line lengths appear odd as in 'Heaven-Haven' with the longer third line or the very long lines of 'Felix Randall'. With Hopkins's system of sprung rhythm, there is no need to make a careful balance between the stressed and unstressed units in a line. His rhythmical method, together with his astonishing use of language, the compound words, the odd comparisons, and his use of alliteration, gives a unique flavour to his poems. Note for example how often the same sound or letter can dominate a line such as the 'i' sound in lines 4–5 of 'Spring'.

A Mini Mind Map will help you to work out the complex ideas in Hopkins's poems.

Activities and brain workers

? Hopkins used compound words like *rollrock* and *flake-doves* to highlight his observation of the world. Look at where you live and make up some compound words of your own. If you live in a town you might be 'road-circled' for example. When you have made up a number of compound words write a poem using them.

? Hopkins uses other technical devices, such as alliteration (*swift, slow; sweet, sour*). Compose some lines of your own that could refer to the work of a blacksmith like Felix Randall. First re-read the poem to help you remember the kind of man he was.

? 'Inversnaid' is a very visual poem of a wild landscape. Write a short prose piece describing any landscape you know using your own compound words to give it an immediacy.

now take a break — listen to some music or have a drink before continuing

T. S. Eliot

Thomas Stearns Eliot (1888–1965) was born in St Louis, USA, and educated at Harvard, the Sorbonne (France) and Merton College, Oxford. In 1914 he met the American poet Ezra Pound, who helped him edit his early poems and get them published. It was Pound who urged him to settle in England, where he became a British citizen in 1927. He also joined the Church of England.

In 1915 he married Vivien Haigh-Wood, but it was an unhappy marriage, partly due to his wife's mental and physical ill health. He taught for a brief period and in 1917 worked for Lloyds Bank. Eight years later he joined the book publishers Faber & Faber, where he built up an important poetry list. In 1922 he published a long poem, 'The Waste Land', which established his reputation. This important poem had been edited by Ezra Pound and was dedicated to him as *il miglior fabbro* (the better craftsman), in the same year he founded the influential literary magazine *The Criterion*.

Eliot, Pound and a number of other American writers looked for ways to revolutionize English poetry, which they believed had become dull and prosaic. They looked for new models both from the classical world of Greece and Rome and in contemporary French poetry. They were deeply influenced by mediaeval European poets, particularly the great Italian poet Dante (1265–1321). They founded, or were involved with, a number of literary movements between the wars; but above all Eliot and Pound were the father figures of the movement we now call Modernism.

The Modernist movement changed the direction and atmosphere of English poetry for ever, breaking away from traditional rhyme and rhythms in its search for alternative ways of writing. It is difficult now, after more than seventy years, to realize what a profound influence it had on English literature.

As well as writing poetry Eliot was also a dramatist and critic. His best known play is probably *Murder in the Cathedral* (1935).

'Preludes'

This short sequence of linked poems gives an impression of the desolation of urban life at the beginning of the century. The drab monotony is reinforced by the poems' time sequence, which takes us around in a circle from evening (I), morning (II), night and morning (III) and evening again with the end of another working day (IV). It has a cinematic quality about it, which is one of the features of Modernism. Events are set out almost without comment, as if one is watching a film. Although it is about a bustling modern city, there are no crowds or real people. Even though it is carefully constructed one gets the feeling that it has been casually thrown together. This is partly due to the rhymes and their pattern. Much of the rhyming is apparently random, but in fact it is scrupulously controlled to give an impression of chance, the haphazard quality of a city.

The sequence of linked poems is a Modernist invention. In one sense it is a long poem with the tedious linking material cut out. It is similar to the rapid changes that can happen in a film. ✪ Why do you think Eliot has used the name of a musical form for the title?

SECTION I

A brief description of the end of another working day in a great city. The poem creates an atmosphere rather than actually saying that the writer finds the winter evening depressing. ✪ What is the weather like in this section?

Note how apparently random things like smells, scraps, chimney-pots and a cab-horse are used to create the impression of urban decay. The phrase *vacant lots* is an American expression meaning empty areas of land, often used for dumping rubbish.

SECTION II

It is the early morning of the next day, with its *faint stale smells of beer* recalling the previous night. Note the use of *stale*, which also means a horse's urine, so reminding the reader of cab-horses. Workers are getting up in the *thousand furnished rooms* and are preparing for another day. Some will stop at the coffee-stands on their way to work. The whole atmosphere of the piece is one of apathy, as the daily round begins yet again. ❂ *Shades* is an American word. What is the English equivalent?

SECTION III

This shows one of the inhabitants of the dismal world of bedsitters. She is not named. All we know about her is that she has had a restless night and has watched the morning getting lighter. The light flickering in under the shutters and the sounds of the birds in the gutters give her an unusual impression of the street outside – one that *the street hardly understands*. She is sitting on the bed removing the curling papers from her hair. These were used in Eliot's day to make ringlets. There is something cruel in Eliot's depiction of this unnamed woman who lives without hope or expectation. The mention of her yellow feet and dirty hands all help to demean her. The poem expresses the isolation of people in a bustling modern city. They are just cogs in the machine. ❂ What do you think is meant by the *thousand sordid images*? Where else in the poem does Eliot use this number? Eliot depicts her as being completely alone despite the fact that she lives in a huge city. It is this kind of isolation that leads to a spiritual despair.

SECTION IV

We are again at the end of the working day with men returning from factories and offices, buying an evening newspaper and smoking, the simple pleasures allowed to them. Eliot sees the urban poor as a downtrodden creature (*... some gentle/ Infinitely suffering thing*). He shows no concern for ordinary people and turns away laughing. ❂ What do you think has blackened the streets?

'Morning at the Window'

This covers similar ground to 'Preludes', with the poet looking down from his window at the street below, in particular into the areas in front of the basement kitchens from where, through open windows, he hears cooks and servants preparing breakfast. Occasionally a passer-by sees him and he receives an embarrassed smile. Just as in the 'Preludes' it is the

bleakness and inscrutability of the city that is being expressed.
✪ How do you know that the streets are muddy?

'Journey of the Magi'

The Magi are the three wise men. In this poem one of them,
now an old man, tells the story of his journey to Bethlehem to
visit the Christ child in the stable. Although the journey was
difficult, the speaker explains that he would do it again even
though the birth of Christ has swept away the old certainties
and gods that he understood.

✝ Eliot wrote this poem around the time that he became a
member of the Church of England and it marks his
growing concern with the problems of religion, and possibly
his own religious doubts.

In the first section we get a straightforward description of the
difficulties in making such a journey 2,000 years ago. ✪ List
some of the problems encountered. In the second stanza there
is a change as the Magi come nearer in time and place to the
birth of Christ. The journey becomes easier as they enter a
✝ *temperate valley*. There is a hint of Christ's betrayal in
the line *six hands at an open door dicing for pieces of
silver*, as Judas betrayed Christ for pieces of silver and the
Roman soldiers played dice for Christ's robe at the crucifixion.
Good poems work on several levels at one time by referring to
things that the reader already knows. The reader brings to the
poem this additional information because of Eliot's allusion to
the Crucifixion.

In the final stanza the old man recognizes that Christ's birth
signals the new religion and that it will replace his safe world
of understandable, but heathen, gods. Although he is unable to
believe in Christianity he knows that he witnessed something
of great significance and now back in his own country the
memory of Christ's birth causes him to find his own world one
of *alien people clutching their gods*. He is tired of a life that he
realizes has little worth and would welcome his own death
I should be glad of another death. ✪ Why do you think that
the speaker cannot change and accept Christianity?

'Rannoch, by Glencoe'

This and the following poem are IV and III in a series of five poems called 'Landscapes'. This one deals with the bleak moorland in Argyll where the *soft sky* almost touches the *soft moor*; but behind the description Eliot is recalling the fact that in the pass of Glencoe the Campbell clan treacherously murdered many of the rival MacDonald clan in 1692. The poem suggests that the barren landscape still bears an impression of the massacre. ✪ What do you think Eliot means by *broken steel*? How could it be languorous? He adds to the area's desolation by showing that the landscape is almost incapable of supporting wildlife, the *crow starves*, and even the stag is there only to be hunted. This harshness recalls the treacherous slaughter that took place in the glen.

'Usk'

This refers to the Welsh river and, as above, the landscape that it passes through is steeped in history and legend, particularly the stories of King Arthur and his Knights of the Round Table. Phrases like *The white hart*, and the *hermit's chapel* point to events from these stories. The lance in line 4 could refer to the one that pierced Christ's side on the cross. This lance is one of the potent symbols in the Arthurian stories about the search for the Holy Grail. ✪ Does the poem create an atmosphere rather than stating an exact idea? Eliot implies that we should not be tricked into believing something just because a historical event took place in the vicinity. We will not find the *white hart* now. We must make our own choice about how we live, *Where the roads dip and where the roads rise/ Seek only there*. It is up to everyone to find his own path to salvation. ✪ What are the *old enchantments*?

'A Cooking Egg'

This is a poem full of references to other poems, **parody** (imitation of other styles of writing or speech), and quotations. It constantly refers to people, places and things that today's reader may not understand. For example ABC's were popular teashops of Eliot's day, the letters stood for the Aerated Bread Company, and they would have been found in areas of London like Kentish Town and Golder's Green. Sir Alfred

Mond was a wealthy industrialist with an interest in literature. Madame Blavatsky was the founder of a religious or spiritual organization called Theosophy. Both were well known in Eliot's time, just as footballers and pop stars are in ours.

A 'cooking egg' means one that might not be fresh and so was used for mixing into other ingredients. The French quotation is the opening lines of 'Le Testament', a famous poem by François Villon (1431–85), one of the poets who influenced Eliot.

The first two stanzas describe a room in Eliot's day, probably a drawing room, as Pipit is there with her reading and knitting. On the mantelpiece leaning against representations of her family is a Dance Invitation. We have a snapshot of this room. Daguerreotypes are early photographs, and it was popular in Victorian times to have silhouettes made of friends and relatives. Photography was not yet available to ordinary people. We are not told who Pipit is, but the description of her drawing room suggests that she is somewhat old-fashioned and staid. She is probably married and may be based on Eliot's first wife.

In the second section, marked by a series of dots, the poet fantasizes about what might have happened with his life and could still happen in heaven. He might have made money with Sir Alfred Mond, or married someone sexually exciting, intellectually stimulating but dangerous like Lucretia Borgia. She was a patron of the arts in sixteenth-century Italy and part of a family infamous for treachery, murder and intrigue. In Eliot's day she was a symbol of the exciting, sinister female. His spiritual needs might have been served by Madame Blavatsky's new movement, or by Piccarda de Donati, who was renowned for her gentleness and is mentioned here as a contrast to Lucretia Borgia. She is both historical and a character in Dante's poem *The Divine Comedy*, where she resides in paradise. Dante (1265–1321) is another influence on Eliot.

With the third section, marked again by a series of dots, we are back in the real world with Pipit. Here Eliot considers the shallowness of modern life, or as he puts it, the *penny world*. There is perhaps just a glimmer of hope that there could be something better, in the line *Where are the eagles and the trumpets*; but it is fairly despairing. ❂ What do you think Eliot means by *the eagles and trumpets*?

The poem explores a lacklustre bourgeois life. The first section uses the lifeless drawing room to symbolize its sterility. The middle hints at the missed opportunities. There may be a parody of the biblical Psalm 23 with the repeated *I shall not want*. The third section shows the failure to grasp any real reward – there are no triumphs, *no eagles or trumpets*. All that can be hoped for is to avoid *the red-eyed scavengers*. This may refer to the working classes, who are creeping towards the bastions of the middle classes from even drearier suburbs like Kentish Town.

Modernist poets like Eliot often used their specialized knowledge of literature and history in a symbolic way. The mention of a character is meant to evoke all that they stood for. This shorthand system works well if the reader knows that Coriolanus is a Roman general noted for his arrogance and that Sir Philip Sidney (1554–86) was a poet, soldier and courtier considered to represent all the best qualities of his period. ❂ In the last stanza who are the weeping multitudes and why do they droop?

'Triumphal March'

This is one of a pair of poems called 'Coriolan' that examines political themes. The title alludes to Shakespeare's play *Coriolanus*. The poem was written in 1931 when various dictators ruled Europe, most notably Mussolini in Italy. It was a period of political unrest that in two more years would see Adolf Hitler and Antonio Salazar as virtual dictators in Germany and Portugal. Like much of Eliot's poetry this poem is filled with allusions and quotes. For example, the catalogue of military equipment is transcribed from the list that the Germans destroyed or surrendered at the end of the First World War.

The poem's content is fairly straightforward. An unnamed hero is having a ceremonial procession in the manner of an ancient Roman triumph. Eliot gives it a modern touch by including non-military groups in the parade. First come the symbols of power, *flags*, *oakleaves*, *eagles*, then the military equipment that the hero has captured. Eliot gives it an absurd quality by the sheer numbers involved. It would be almost impossible to parade *5,800,000 rifles and carbines*. ✪ What do you think is meant by the *eagles*? The crowd waits anticipating the hero. They know it will be a long wait as they have brought stools and food (*sausages*). Like the range of military equipment there is something mildly ridiculous about a sausage. Then the great man rides past on his horse and the crowd is disappointed that he appears so ordinary. The magnificent cavalcade makes its way to the temple to give thanks, presumably for some military victory. Now to those opening symbols of *stone*, *bronze*, *steel*, *oakleaves* is added *dust*, the symbol for mortality. The hero may be a great general or statesman, but he will die just as surely as anyone else.

There is a sense of disappointment amongst the onlookers once the parade has passed. They have not learned anything of gravity from the display of military might, nor can they remember how many eagles or trumpets they saw. The poem ends with the onlookers talking about inconsequential things. There is the overheard conversation about taking Cyril to church. Someone asks for a light for a cigarette The bell is both part of the church service, rung at the consecration of the host, and a reference to the street-sellers of crumpets who rang a bell in Eliot's day. ✪ In what city do you think this procession could have taken place?

'Macavity: The Mystery Cat'

This is a much lighter piece. Eliot wrote light and some bawdy verse, much of it in letters to friends and not for publication. This and several more poems are gathered together in a book called *Old Possum's Book of Practical Cats*. 'Possum' was one of the names that Eliot's friend Ezra Pound called him. The musical play 'Cats' is based on the book.

The poem is easy to read and understand. Eliot pretends that this somewhat shabby cat is really a master criminal. Even in a light piece like this the cat's name is important. 'Cavity' suggests a cave, or a hole, places where such a cat might hide ✪ Why do you think Macavity is blamed for so many things? Make a list of them. ✪ What colour is he?

Revision points

Eliot writes about a number of crises that came together in the early part of the twentieth century. These are political and also spiritual. On the political side there was the rise of authoritarian states, as well as the growing power of the working classes via the new socialist movements. Ordinary people had witnessed the hideousness of trench warfare and no longer had complete faith in traditional leaders. The spread of education led people to question orthodox Christianity. The relatively new discipline of psychoanalysis had percolated down to the general public, spreading further doubts and helping to wipe away previously accepted standards and beliefs. Eliot was writing at a time of uncertainty and although many people searched for new religious and political truths, he saw these as hopeless and despairing, preferring, in his own case, to embrace the Church of England.

Eliot and the other Modernists altered the shape, diction and atmosphere of poetry. They deliberately changed the traditional way of writing by using a less formal verse form. They learned from European poets and particularly painters. Many famous Modernist poems use collage, a technique adapted from the painters of the period, who added things like newspaper cuttings, bus tickets and adverts to their paintings to give an immediacy to their work. In 'Triumphal March' Eliot uses snippets of French, quotes from other poems, makes lists and puts all these unrelated pieces together to create an atmosphere, an impression of the event.

The verse itself looks different from that of previous poems. Consider the varying line lengths in 'Triumphal March' for example. When you read some of the poems you will notice sudden changes in pace and rhythm; they are there for a purpose. One of the things that the Modernist writers said they wanted to do was to break the iambic rhythm of poetry, to 'compose in the sequence of the musical phrase, not in sequence of a metronome', as one of them put it. In other words they thought that there could be an in-built rhythm in a phrase and that poems could be composed of them, without the lines relying on a series of repeated stresses (the regularity of a metronome). Eliot's experiments led to the kind of poetry that we have today. He has to be considered as one of the most important poets of the twentieth century.

Activities and brain workers

? In 'A Cooking Egg' Eliot uses historical characters to represent certain ideas or conditions, Lucretia Borgia representing a sexually exciting woman and Coriolanus a military leader noted for his arrogance. Suggest modern equivalents for them. Discuss this with your friends.

? This Mini Mind Map is for 'Rannoch, by Glencoe'. Read the poem again and make your own Mind Map to help you remember that particular landscape and poem. Then make a mini Mind Map for 'Usk'

? In 'Morning at the Window' Eliot writes about what he sees and hears when he looks out of his window. Write a poem or a short piece of prose describing what you would see if you looked out of your window in the morning.

? Write a brief description of Macavity's character.

take a break to phone a friend; but don't discuss your work or school – just have a rest before continuing

Robert Frost

Robert Lee Frost (1874–1963) was born in San Francisco. His father died when he was 10 and he was taken by his mother to the farming area of Massachusetts, so as to be close to his paternal grandparents. He did a variety of jobs, including editing a country newspaper and teaching. In 1912 he came to England with his wife. Here he published his first two collections of poems, *A Boy's Will* (1913) and *North of Boston* (1914). At the outbreak of the First World War he returned to the USA, settling in New Hampshire, where he farmed. With the publication of further books of poetry his reputation was established and he was able to support himself by college teaching.

Although Frost lived a long and somewhat uneventful life, it was one touched by family tragedy. In 1934 his youngest child died and a few years later his wife had a fatal heart attack. His son committed suicide in 1940.

He is a popular poet who wrote about country life in simple and accessible language. His dramatic monologues and pastoral poems have made some critics regard him as a twentieth-century Wordsworth.

'The Pasture'

This describes two of the things that Frost the farmer is going to do. It is almost as if he is talking to his reader rather than writing a poem. This colloquial way of writing is one of Frost's characteristic strengths. The content of this poem is about ordinary tasks and goes to show that poems do not have to be about momentous thoughts, emotions or events.
❂ Who do you think Frost is speaking to with his *You come too?*

'Mowing'

Another description of one of the many tasks that farmers had to do in the past. Frost finds pleasure in cutting grass with a scythe and thinks about the sound it makes; but he does not look for any deeply intellectual response – cutting the grass is just a job that has to be done. ❂ Why is there no sound from the wood? Note the careful rhyming here. It might help to write down the pattern using letters.

'Mending Wall'

In spring Frost the farmer has to repair the dry stone wall that separates his land from a neighbour's. The wall has been damaged by winter weather *That sends the frozen-ground-swell under it/ And spills the upper boulders*, as well as by hunters who have removed stones so that their dogs can run freely to catch rabbits. He lets his neighbour know that he is wall-mending and together they patrol the wall making repairs, each keeping to his own side and only replacing stones that have fallen on their side. ❂ Describe the shape of some of the stones. Although his neighbour says, *Good fences make good neighbours* Frost wonders why the wall is really needed. Neither has livestock that could wander on to the other's land. ❂ What do they grow on their land? He mentions this to his neighbour, who does not comment, but just continues with the repairing *bringing a stone grasped firmly by the top* and repeating, as his father had done before, *Good fences make good neighbours*. Although Frost does not care whether the wall is rebuilt, his neighbour is keen to re-establish the boundary. It as if the neighbour needs to put a barrier between himself and Frost. This may be something that the neighbour has learned from his father as he repeats the words *Good fences make good neighbours.* ✪ Try drawing a section of dry stone wall showing the stones' shapes.

The poem's rhythm imitates the slow, meticulous work of rebuilding, as Frost presents each item in the process. This slowly unwinding logic might appear dry if it were not punctuated by humour such as Frost's comments on a precariously replaced stone, '*Stay where you are until our backs are turned!*'

'After Apple-picking'

Frost the apple farmer has had the bumper crop that he wanted; but he is tired and fed up with picking apples. The small farmer in Frost's day used a ladder to hand pick every apple. There was no machinery to help. ✪ Why does his foot ache? Which lines explain this? There is nothing idyllic or romantic about this harvest – it has been hard work. ✪ How many apples does he say he has picked? What happened to any apple that fell?

The poem conveys Frost's weariness with the constant reminder of the colour and shape of apples. This is reinforced by the use of rhyme. The irregular rhyme pattern and the variation in line lengths help to give an impression of the work as he stretches to reach *Magnified apples* that *appear and disappear* as the leaves and branches reveal another cluster.

The poem starts with the end of his working day, although it does mention its beginning with the reference to finding ice on the drinking trough. His ladder is still in the trees and he knows that he might have missed a few apples, but he is *done with apple picking now*. He is exhausted physically and mentally by his labour and is ready for sleep. He thinks about the woodchuck (a marmot, a North American rodent that lives in a burrow), that has already hibernated (*his/ long sleep*). Frost hopes that his sleep will have some meaningfulness, but he realizes that it will just be ordinary, *some human sleep*, in spite of his heroic activity.

'An Old Man's Winter Night'

An unnamed old man on a cold winter's night goes into his cellar, lamp in hand; but when he gets there he has forgotten what he went there for and he returns. ✪ What is in the cellar? Draw a picture of the old man's cellar. He sits beside his stove falling asleep and is hardly disturbed by a log slipping. Usually in Frost's poems we get the impression of the poet almost talking to us, as he explains what it is like to be a farmer, for example. Here Frost offers a series of images starting with the cold outside the farm. The window is just beginning to frost over (*thin frost, almost in separate stars*), then the familiar sounds *of trees and crack of branches, common things*, and finally the old man dozing by his fire. The whole poem is cinematic in construction, with the camera looking through the frosting window at the old man (*All out-of-doors looked darkly in at him*).

Frost ends his story by wondering how the old man can cope not just with age, but with the obvious isolation and loneliness. As in much of Frost's poetry there is a feeling of acceptance, of the inevitability of a certain way of life. The progression to old age is as natural as all the other things encountered in life.

'Birches'

Frost observes how some birch trees are permanently bent as their lighter upper branches have been damaged by the weight of ice and storms. He compares them to long-haired girls kneeling with their hair thrown in front of them.

These particular trees have been marred by harsh weather, but Frost prefers to think that they have been bent over by some boy swinging from the higher, flexible branches. He remembers that he used to play such games (*So was I once myself a swinger of birches*). This imaginary boy – or it might be a real boy, or even Frost himself – would climb up the stronger lower branches, cling onto the upper ones, and, jumping off (*flung outward, feet first*), let the tree swing him down to the ground. Frost describes the game in great detail, almost as if he is remembering his own youth, the youth of a boy *too far from town to learn baseball*. ✪ What happens to the ice-covered trees after rain?

Thinking about these childhood things reminds him of the difficulties of adult life (*It's when I'm weary of considerations*) and for a moment he wishes that he could again climb the birches and play, like a child. It is only a momentary thought for he soon realizes that one has to face daily responsibilities. There is perhaps a note of defiance in the last two lines that appears at odds with adult responsibilities.

'Dust of Snow'

This elegant poem describes a crow perching on a branch and knocking feathery snow on to the poet below. This amusing accident changes the poet's mood for the better. There may be some significance in Frost's choice of tree. In the USA it is a type of conifer whereas in England hemlock is a poisonous plant, associated with suicide and murder, so this may give a clue to his previous mood. The poem is a sharp depiction of a single event. It is almost photographic. ✪ Try to picture it in your mind's eye.

'Stopping by Woods on a Snowy Evening'

The poem records Frost's pleasure in pausing to look at the wintry landscape. His thoughts are about his horse's surprise at stopping, and other musings about who might own these woods. ✪ How does the horse show its surprise? Frost is enchanted by the beauty of the landscape, but realizes that he cannot stop long as he has things to do and there is still a long way to go (*But I have promises to keep/ And miles to go before I sleep*). Note how the rhythm imitates the horse's slow plod.

Frost reiterates his belief that we have a liability to others and that simple duties like being on time and keeping promises are important.

'Two Look at Two'

A pair of lovers are walking up a mountain path and are reluctant to return in the twilight down the rough path. Their progress is halted by a tumbled-down wall which makes them realize that now they have to turn back. Taking one last look in the fading light, they are surprised by a female deer (*doe*) which stares back at them. Because they are standing still the deer is not frightened. She sighs and wanders off. The couple are thrilled by the event and are about to leave when the male deer (*buck*) appears. Like the doe the buck is not frightened by the unmoving couple. Frost imagines that the buck is thinking that the couple are hardly alive because of their immobility (*Why don't you make some motion?/ Or give some sign of life?*). They almost break this magical moment by reaching out to the deer, but they refrain and the buck wanders off. Thus the 'twos' of the title have looked at each other. For the humans it has been close to a mystical experience. They stand entranced for a few more moments seeing the deer as a kind of mirror image of their own love. ❂ How do the couple realize that they have seen two separate deer?

Note how the poem slowly builds to its climax. Frost presents a series of small events that lead to the appearance of the doe, which could be the end of the poem, then he adds the even more exciting entrance of the buck.

'Tree at My Window'

Frost imagines a connection between himself and the tree, particularly when both have been troubled, the tree by wind (*I have seen you taken and tossed*) and the poet by unexplained problems (*when I was taken and swept/ And all but lost*). Although he can address the tree in this way Frost does not give in to romantic thoughts and the tree remains essentially a tree even though it can see the poet (*You have seen me*). ❂ What is meant by *sash* in the first stanza?

This lyrical poem expresses the romantic belief that the natural world can mirror our inner nature. In the last stanza Frost draws a parallel between the tree's concerns with wind and weather and his own troubled thoughts: the 'inner' and 'outer' weather.

'Unharvested'

Smelling something sweet the poet looks over a wall to discover that an apple tree has shed all its apples in a *circle of solid red*. We are not told why this particular tree has been unharvested, but are aware that this unplanned event pleases Frost (*May something go always unharvested*). Although it is a natural occurrence, Frost hints at something more profound with the association of *an apple fall* and the spiritual fall of man with *As complete as the apple had given man*. He does not develop the idea, but it remains a reminder of humankind's frailty. ✪ Why is there no theft in *smelling their sweetness*? The poem also expresses Frost's joy in the unexpected.

'The Silken Tent'

This is a more involved poem than those that have dealt with rural life and farming. This metaphorical comparison of a silken tent with a woman's character has something of the intellectual exercise about it. This is strengthened by the uncharacteristic language and the fact that the 14 lines are one sentence. The main content of the poem would appear to be that a woman, like a tent, can be both free and bound. No single guyrope actually holds the tent; but in the *capriciousness of summer air* a slight wind reveals that the tent is securely held. ✪ What do you think is meant by *signifies the sureness of the soul*? How can a woman be both free and bound?

Revision points

Frost reminds us of the Romantic poets because of his relationship with the countryside. He presents us with a simple world that is governed by the necessary tasks in a farmer's life, mowing, mending walls, harvesting for example. This naïve view of the world also touches his other poems. But unlike the Romantics he presents these tasks without any moral comment and uses a language that is close to everyday speech. In many of his poems we have the sense that he is talking directly to us. Frost could be seen as a modern-day Wordsworth, but it is worth remembering that Frost was a working farmer, whereas Wordsworth lived a somewhat sheltered life as a poet.

Frost's great strength, and the thing that makes us read his poems with pleasure, is his style. He creates the impression that we can hear his voice talking to us, or to himself and because of this we can overhear his thoughts. We get a strong feeling of the man and how his mind works.

There are poems like 'Birches' where memory and the imagination play a part; but in general he presents small events that offer insights into our humanity. He constantly reminds us that the daily rituals such as mending walls, clearing out a spring and mowing bring with them a moral responsibility.

A Mind Map will help you to remember the detail in Frost's poems. It might also help to sort out the elements in an involved poem like 'The Silken Tent'.

Activities and brain workers

? A number of Frost's poems are about a small farmer's daily and routine tasks. Go through his poems and make a list of these things. Are they all still necessary tasks for the modern farmer?

? 'Mending Wall' is one of Frost's most famous poems and yet he half suggests that it is a waste of his time. Why do you think he mends the wall ? Try writing a short poem of your own about a task that you have to do, but think is unnecessary. It might be something at school or at home, such as keeping your room tidy.

? Copy out 'Dust of Snow' making the words quite big, or photocopy it, enlarging the size. Then cut up the paper so that you have one word on each cut piece. Put the pieces in a hat or box, shake them about, then tip them out on your work surface. Now, without looking at the poem again, arrange them so that they make sense.

? Read 'Birches' again and then write a description of what it might be like to climb a birch tree, grab its upper branches and let the tree lower you to the ground.

now take a break before starting on the next poet

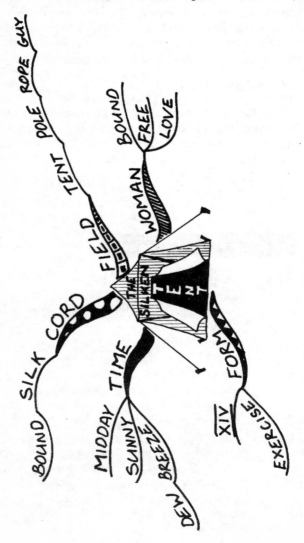

R. S. Thomas

Ronald Stuart Thomas was born in Cardiff in 1913. He was educated at St Michael's College, Llandaff and University College, Bangor. In 1936 he was ordained as a clergyman in the Church of Wales, and for most of his life he served as a minister to a number of rural parishes. His poetry is almost always about Wales and the isolated communities in which he worked. Although he taught himself Welsh, so as to communicate with his parishioners, his poetry is written exclusively in English. Despite this, in recent years he has been associated with Welsh nationalism.

He published his first book of poetry, *The Stones of the Field*, in 1946 and is still writing and publishing new poems in 1999 (as this guide is being written). His work is characterized by the experience of working in remote communities, where the landscape is harsh and earning a living is difficult. There is something almost savage in his observation of this landscape and its people. He may understand the difficulties of his parishioners, but he rarely offers sympathy. He is an accurate reporter uninvolved in their plight. In consequence his language is plain and rather bleak.

'Tramp'

A tramp knocks on the poet's door and asks for tea. ✪ How does Thomas think the tramp would like his tea? Both have their concerns: the tramp looks at his feet, perhaps worrying about the state of his boots, and Thomas the clergyman looks to the sky concerned about the planes that symbolize the complexity of the modern world (*Of that new world/ We have sworn by*). Thomas compares the condensation trails made by the planes with rafters (*The shining rafters/ Of that new world*). There is probably an allusion here to a famous novel by Aldous Huxley called *Brave New World*, that shows a concern for the future. The final stanza compares how the two men will sleep that night: the tramp in a ditch and Thomas in a bed. The poet wonders whether the tramp's dreams are less haunted than his own. ✪ What do you think haunts Thomas's dreams?

'Song'

These contrasting quatrains give a clue to Thomas's concerns.
The first is enthusiastic about searching for mushrooms and the
second unsentimental about the failure to find any in the harsh
terrain. Although it is called 'Song' there is nothing very lyrical
about the poem. ✪ What do you think *asylum* means here?

'Abersoch'

A snapshot of a moment observed in this small North Wales
fishing town. Thomas can only remember a few things, such as
the girl *Riding her cycle* and the men smoking. There is an
impending storm and Thomas observes the lightning out at sea
and hears the thunder. Note the contrast between the *dinghies
at rest/ On the calm tide* and the storm threatening to break.
Thomas appears to be asking why these few simple things
should leave such a strong impression. ✪ What do you think the
last line means? Does it tell you what the men do for a living?

'An Old Man'

The man is seen taking hesitant steps as he checks to see
whether the wet road is icy. The word *muffled* in the second
line suggests that the man is wearing a scarf, as well as the fact
that his freezing breath looks like a muffler. ✪ Apart from the
title what other lines tell you that he is old? In the man's last
years Thomas wishes that he could have some ease from the
severity of his life. Note the comparison with a tree that
has survived the storm. It is not just people that Thomas
sees as being ground down by the harshness of living; but also
the land itself. The last line suggests that his journey may be
safer when the wintry sun has melted the ice.

'The Evacuee'

This is a compassionate poem looking at a young girl
who has been evacuated to the country during the
Second World War. Many children were saved from the
danger of being bombed and killed in the cities and towns by
being sent to safe rural areas. Their parents could not
accompany them as they were either working or serving in the
armed forces.

The girl wakes up for the first time on the farm and for a moment she is confused by the silence and the fact that she cannot hear any air raid warning sirens. The silence is broken by a cock's crow and the farm comes to life with all its other noises.

Note how Thomas suggests the countryside with a *loose quilt/ Of leaf patterns* so as you are unsure whether it is a real quilt or just the dappled light on the bed.

In the second stanza she rushes down the stairs to meet the people sitting at the table. ❂ What do you think they are doing there? The final stanza looks back at what happened to her as she grew up on the farm. Thomas is suggesting that growing up in the country is better than living *In the flowerless streets of the drab town.* ❂ What other phrases suggest that the girl benefits from being in the country? Thomas comments on her thinness when she first arrived (*the sticks of limbs*) and how later she put on weight, with her *soft flesh ripening warm as corn.*

During the war nearly all food was rationed, so people could only buy small amounts. Some town dwellers grew vegetables in their gardens, but not everyone had a garden. In the country it was easier to eat well.

'Farm Child'

This picture of a boy born and raised in the country is in contrast to 'The Evacuee'. There is no fear in his eyes as there was dread in the evacuee's. Thomas states that rural life has given the boy a poise and *unconscious grace*, and he knows how his life will turn out. The poem praises the benefits of growing up in the country. There is in the last line a touch of sadness as the boy's grace and knowledge will lead only to the limiting life of a farm labourer. ❂ Draw a Mini Mind Map of all the things that he has in his pockets.

'Soil'

A labourer is working late cutting off the green tops of swedes and mangolds (a kind of beet used for cattle feed). The tops will be used for cattle feed now and the heavy root will be stored for the winter. In the first stanza he is seen almost as a machine as he slowly and systematically works his way down the rows. ❂ What word suggests this? Thomas shows how the man is restrained not just by the field's hedges, but by the fact that he is totally engrossed in his task. Occasionally his knife slips and he cuts himself, but even this does not stop his progress. Thomas hints at something almost pagan when he writes *the blood seeps home/ To the warm soil*, as if in this sacrifice there is some pact between the man and the earth that sustains him.

'Children's Song'

This shows that the world of children is totally remote and isolated from parents and adults. There is no way that they can enter into it, not even if they stoop or get *on hands and knees*. A child's world is more than just its smallness, it is a place of innocence, where *life is still asleep*. Underlying this apparently plain observation is a lament for the loss of innocence that happens to everyone as they reach adulthood. ✪ What is meant by the 'centre' that adults cannot find?

'The Village'

This tiny place hardly seems to have any importance; *a black dog/ Cracking his fleas* appears to be the only thing that is happening. The village is isolated and probably in decline (*the green tide/ Of grass creeping perpetually nearer*). The sudden appearance of the girl moving through the village reveals that there is life here, meaningful life for the people who live and work there. It is just as important to them as the Greek philosopher Plato's vision of the world. Thomas may be using the girl as a symbol for growth, as when she becomes a woman and has children, she will be responsible for the village's next generation. Note how the rhythm conveys a sense of isolation and emptiness. ✪ What are the *bland day's two dimensions*?

'The Poacher'

A vivid description of another character who was once a traditional part of the countryside. He is almost invisible as he blends into his surroundings. Thomas is perhaps suggesting that the poacher and nature are in co-operation. ✪ Which lines suggest this? Thomas does not condemn poaching – he sees it as part of rural life. The poacher is shown as a decent man, but there are hints at a darker side to his nature. The *steel comb* suggests a trap or snare. *Familiar* may allude to a witch's familiar, an animal, usually a cat or dog, that is supposed to accompany witches. Thomas may offer the poacher a *frank greeting* but he is also aware of this menacing side to his personality. Note the use of words and phrases that suggest the poacher's wariness. ✪ Write these down.

'Cynddylan on a Tractor'

In contrast to some of Thomas's rather bleak looks at rural life there is something almost comic about the depiction of Cynddylan (pronounced Cunthullan, with *thu* as in 'the'), especially when he drives through his farmyard *scattering hens*. The tractor will free him from back-breaking manual labour, but it also separates the peasant farmer from the soil. The threat that increased mechanization will destroy the balance between man and nature is one of Thomas's concerns. Thomas writes that Cynddylan is *a new man now, part of the machine*, again proposing that machinery is somehow dehumanizing and breaks the ties with the natural world. ✪ What do you think has emptied the woods *Of foxes and squirrels and bright jays*?

'Evans'

Thomas in his role of a parish priest is visiting a sick farmer in an isolated and bleak farm. Look at the words Thomas uses to increase our feeling of destitution (*bare, gaunt, black, cold, dark, stark, rain, stranded, lonely*). The fact that there is only one tree, and that it is *weather-tortured* and dripping in the rain helps to create an atmosphere of desolation. As in most of his poems Thomas does not offer any comment, he just describes, this time in some detail, the situation he encounters. Even the last line shares this barrenness as *shore* suggests isolation. There is a hopelessness in this poem as Thomas in his role of priest cannot do anything to alleviate the farmer's suffering. It is interesting to compare this poem with Hopkins's 'Felix Randall' noting the difference in outlook between the two parish priests. ✪ Think about the striking image in the last two lines. What does it suggest about Evans, and how Thomas sees his relationship with him?

'A Day in Autumn'

This depiction of a calm autumn day is to be remembered, as winter with its terrible weather will soon sweep through the Welsh hills again. If they can hold the image of a calm day in the mind it will help the inhabitants to get through the cold, wind and rain that will soon be with them. Note how he compares this idea with warm clothing: *something to wear*. ✪ What do you think is meant by the *lawn's mirror*?

'The Hill Farmer Speaks'

This is an uncomplicated poem stating that however harsh the conditions the hill farmer endures, he still has the same feelings and desires as the rest of us: *I am a man like you*. He may be *stripped of love/ And thought and grace*, but his basic humanity is revealed by his concern for his livestock. The farmer and his animals are in a sense a community (*The pig is my friend*) resisting the worst that nature throws at them. They are yoked together. He starves if his ewes go hungry.

Thomas lets the farmer speak directly to us. He does not get in the way or comment. ❂ What impression do we get of the farmer's mind from the lines *stray thoughts pass/ Over the floor of my wide skull*?

'A Blackbird Singing'

Thomas wonders why such a marvellous song should be uttered by a bird that is associated with *dark places*. Another level of meaning is introduced by the allusion to alchemy in the first stanza with *the notes'/ Ore were changed to rare metal*. The alchemists believed that they could turn lead into gold with the use of something they called the Philosopher's Stone. ❂ Which part of the bird does Thomas suggest performs a similar task? In the second stanza Thomas involves the reader by reminding us that we too have heard the blackbird's song on a mild evening.

The final stanza develops the deeper meaning by suggesting that the blackbird shares the memories of all its predecessors; but is still able to present its song *with new tears*. ❂ Whom do you think is addressed in the second stanza?

'Lore'

In contrast to the gloom in some of Thomas's poems here he extols the life of a rumbustious 85-year-old farm labourer who has always worked hard, but is still full of enthusiasm for living. ❂ What does Thomas say has kept him going in the harsh conditions? Once again Thomas hints that traditional ways are best, as Job Davies would rather use a scythe than a machine. ❂ What do you think is meant by *dream small*?

Revision points

Thomas was for most of his working life a parish priest ministering to the isolated areas of Wales. Although he rarely expresses anger at the harshness of life in such places, it is easy to feel his sense of frustration, his inability to do much good in these circumstances. His diction (use of language) is harsh and bleak as he gives us an uncritical picture of people and places. His view of this world is unsentimental. He does not reprove or offer any solutions, neither political nor religious. In some cases his characters have a stoicism and fierce pride as they struggle with the weather and harsh conditions. He shows us a stubborn humanity, often suggesting that there is something almost mystical connecting these hill farmers with their land.

Activities and brain workers

? Mini Mind Maps are a useful way to familiarize yourself with a poem. Here is one for 'Abersoch' but some important items have been omitted. Complete the Mini Mind Map in such a way that it will help you to remember the poem. Don't forget that drawings and colour will help.

? In 'The Hill Farmer Speaks' we have a description of harsh rural life; but it is not written in a farmer's language; Thomas is the interpreter. Read the poem again and then write a short prose passage as if you really are a farmer. Use his kind of language.

? The following people and characters are all mentioned in Thomas's poems. Without referring to the book, write down the title of the poem for each of the following. Use the boxes opposite.

Tramp

⬚

Job Davies

⬚

Poacher

⬚

Girl on a bicycle

⬚

Village boy

⬚

Man cutting mangolds

⬚

Plato

⬚

Read 'The Poacher' again and write a prose description of the man.

now take a long break — you've earned it!

TOPICS FOR DISCUSSION AND BRAINSTORMING

It may sometimes be difficult to understand a poem completely, as you are reading complex language that often only hints at its underlying meaning. One useful way to study poems is with friends – even those who have perhaps read the poem only once.

Start by looking at the various elements that make up a particular poem. Ask yourself and your friend some of the following questions. When was it written? Does the poet's background or profession have any influence? Does it rhyme? Is there a pattern to the rhymes? Is there a similar rhythm throughout the poem? Does the rhythm enhance the content? Does it tell a story? Are there the same number of lines in each stanza? Who is speaking in the poem? Does the language used suggest any emotion? What does the title tell you? What is the poet saying, and do you agree with it? Did you like the poem? Did you learn anything from it?

Don't worry if some ideas seem silly at first. You will be able to reject them or modify them during your discussion. It is important to explore your own thinking and to brainstorm in this way. If your friend thinks an idea is crazy then try to convince him or her of its reasonableness. This kind of session will help you to think creatively and you will also be storing up ideas to help you with exam questions.

When you have considered the above, draw a Mind Map of your conclusions showing the technical points about the poem's construction and what you think it means.

TOPICS

1 To what extent is memory an important factor in Wordsworth's poems?
2 What do you think Blake achieves by the questions in many of his poems?
3 Consider the extracts from narrative poems by Keats and suggest how you might write them as a television script.

4 Write a description or draw a portrait of Hopkins's 'Felix Randall'.

5 Discuss how T. S. Eliot represents ordinary people in his poems.

6 Examine Robert Frost's language and consider whether it indicates that he is an American.

7 Compare R. S. Thomas's and T. S. Eliot's portrayal of working people.

8 To what extent is memory an important factor in Wordsworth's poems?

9 Describe the character of Lucy in Wordworth's 'Lucy Poems'. What do you think she might have been like?

10 What do you think Blake achieves by the questions in many of his poems?

11 Blake questions orthodox Christianity and the way the country is ruled; if he was alive today what do you think his poems might be about.

12 Consider the extracts from narrative poems by Keats and suggest how you might write them as a television script.

13 Why do you think Keats sets some of his poems in a mythical or medieval period?

14 Write a description or draw a portrait of Hopkins' 'Felix Randall'.

15 In 'Pied Beauty' Hopkins lists a number of two coloured things. Think about some more that he could have included.

16 Hopkins' poems look and sound different from most of the other poems in this anthology, one reason is his use of rhyme. What other devices are involved?

17 Discuss how T.S. Eliot represents ordinary people in his poems.

18 Both Eliot and Wordsworth write about lonely individuals; but there is a difference in presentation. What do you think this is?

19 Examine Robert Frost's language and consider whether it indicates that he is an American.

20 Consider the line breaks in Frost's poems and note how they recreate the rhythm of hard labour. Find examples of these in poems like 'After Apple-picking' and 'Mending Wall'.

21 Both Frost and R.S. Thomas write about small farmers, yet there is a great difference in their depiction of this life. Can you find any similarities, and if so, what are they?

22 Compare R.S. Thomas' and T.S. Eliot's portrayal of working people.

In all your study, in coursework, and in exams, be aware of the following:

- **Characterization** – the characters and how we know about them (e.g. what they say and do, how the author describes them), their relationships, and how they develop.
- **Plot and structure** – what happens and how it is organized into parts or episodes.
- **Setting and atmosphere** – the changing scene and how it reflects the story (e.g. a rugged landscape and storm reflecting a character's emotional difficulties).
- **Style and language** – the author's choice of words, and literary devices such as imagery, and how these reflect the mood.
- **Viewpoint** – how the story is told (e.g. through an imaginary narrator, or in the third person but through the eyes of one character – 'She was furious – how dare he!').
- **Social and historical context** – influences on the author (see 'Background' in this guide).

Develop your ability to:

- Relate **detail** to **broader content, meaning and style**.
- Show understanding of the author's **intentions, technique and meaning** (brief and appropriate comparisons with other works by the same author will gain marks).
- Give **personal response and interpretation**, backed up by **examples** and short **quotations**.
- **Evaluate** the author's achievement (how far does the author succeed and why?)

When studying a poem, look for:

- the **emotional tone** (sad, sombre, lively, confused …);
- the **subject** and underlying **theme or themes**;
- the **structure** and **rhyme scheme** (if any), and the use the poet makes of them – remember you will get credit for saying what they are used for, but not for just identifying them;
- effects made by the **choice of words**, and by **imagery**.

THE EXAM ESSAY

PLANNING

You will probably have about an hour for one essay. It is important to spend a few minutes planning it. An excellent way to do this is in the three stages below.

1 **Mind Map** your ideas, without worrying about their order yet.
2 **Order** the relevant ideas (the ones that really relate to the question) by numbering them in the order in which you will write the essay.
3 **Gather** your evidence and short quotes.

You could remember this as the **MOG** technique.

Then compose your essay, allowing five minutes at the end for checking relevance, spelling, grammar, punctuation and the quotes that you have used.

REMEMBER

Stick to the question, and always **back up** your points with evidence in the form of examples and short quotations.

There are two ways of writing quotations in an essay. If it is a one line quote then write it in the body of your essay as follows:

Hopkins tells us something about the farrier's youthful character 'thy more boisterous years'.

If the quotation runs over a line end then use a slash mark (/) to indicate this. When the quotation is more than three lines it is better to centre the quote on its own as follows:

… and unlike Hopkins even humour in 'Cynddylan on a Tractor'.

The clutch curses, but the gears obey
His least bidding, and lo, he's
Out of the farmyard, scattering hens.
Riding to work now as a great man should …

Model answer and plan

The next (and final) chapter consists of an answer to an exam question based on two poets in *A Choice of Poets*, with the Mind Map and essay plan used to write it. Don't be put off if you feel that writing an essay at this stage is too difficult. You'll develop your skills if you work at them. Even if you are reading this the night before the exam, you can easily memorize the MOG technique in order to do your personal best.

The model answer and plan are good examples to follow, but don't just learn them by heart. It's better to pay close attention to the wording of the question you choose to answer in the exam, and allow Mind Mapping to help you think creatively.

Before reading the answer, you might like to do a plan of your own to compare with the example. The numbered points, with comments at the end, show why it's a good answer.

MODEL ANSWER AND ESSAY PLAN

QUESTION

Compare the poetry of Gerard Manley Hopkins and R. S. Thomas, taking into account that they are both priests.

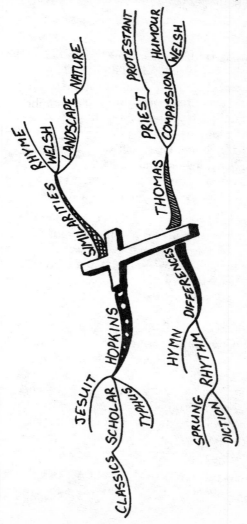

PLAN

1 Hopkins is a Roman Catholic.
2 R. S. Thomas was a minister in the Church of Wales.
3 Both write about nature.
4 Both worked as parish priests.
5 Compare Felix Randall with one of Thomas's characters.
6 Differences.
7 Similarities.
8 Both Welsh speakers.

ESSAY

Religion seems to be the main concern of Hopkins's poems. Many actually praise God, as in 'Pied Beauty' with its opening line, 'Glory be to God'.[1] God is also present in poems about nature and even in a poem ostensibly about the blacksmith Felix Randall: 'Ah well. God rest him all road ever he offended!' Hopkins's Roman Catholicism is evident in the poems that deal with 'original sin'[2] 'It is the blight man was born for,'[1] ('Spring and Fall'). Even if one did not know that Hopkins was a priest the poems would tell you. They constantly refer to God, often exploring the problems of faith.

R. S. Thomas's religion is far less obvious and if one did not already know that he was a minister in the Church of Wales[3] there is very little in the poems that would suggest it. Like Hopkins he also writes about the natural world, but in a very different way. Thomas is an observer and gives us a snapshot of his landscapes 'There was that headland, asleep on the sea,/ The air full of thunder' ('Abersoch'), whereas Hopkins's landscape poems usually praise God for creating them. Another contrast between the two men is their diction.[4] Hopkins uses conventional poetic language, the kind that we expect from poets. Unlike Thomas it is rich with poetic devices such as alliteration,[5] simile and a variety of consonantal and vowel chimes. Thomas's diction is far more colloquial. His 'Kick my arse!' ('Lore') is unexpected from a poet, and especially from a priest. Thomas's vocabulary is down to earth, matter of fact and closer to the language of normal speech.

Both poets use rhyme and again it is Hopkins's rhyme patterns that are conventional. We know when the rhyme is going to come. Thomas on the other hand is far more subtle, sometimes using rhyme to stress a point 'The one tavern and the one shop/ That leads nowhere and fails at the top' ('The Village'); or to round off a poem with a final internal rhyme as in 'On the *brow*'s anvil as the sun does *now*' ('An Old Man').

This contrast is obvious when comparing 'Felix Randall' with any of Thomas's poems about people. Hopkins's language is beautiful and rhythmically inventive. He enjoys writing in set forms like the sonnet.[5] Although it does not look like it because of the long lines, 'Felix Randall' is a sonnet.[5] At a first glance Hopkins's poem looks and sounds far better than any of Thomas's because it has all those things we expect in a poem. Thomas's familiar language, although less artistic, actually tells us more about his characters. All that we really learn about Felix Randall is that he is strong, something we would have guessed because of his trade. Hopkins's poem is more about his own state of mind than that of the blacksmith. Thomas always gives us a marvellous description of his characters, not just their physical appearance, but also an insight into their psychology, 'Rhythm of the long scythe/ Kept this tall frame lithe.' ('Lore') Where Hopkins celebrates his God, Thomas is more concerned with his parishioners.[6] This contrast may have something to do with their social backgrounds. Hopkins is Oxford-educated and later became a professor of Greek, after a short period as a parish priest, whereas Thomas studied at a provincial university and spent most of his life as a priest amongst working people.[3] The difference perhaps between the lofty pursuits of scholarship and the harsh world of a parish priest ministering to impoverished farmers.

In Hopkins's work we are always aware of his spiritual struggle, even in an apparently simple early sonnet[5] like 'Spring'. Here the octave[5] describes the special qualities of the season and the sestet[5] the problems of belief and humankind's inadequacies.

> In Eden garden. – Have, get, before it cloy
> Before it cloud, Christ, lord, and sour with sinning,
> Innocent mind and Mayday in girl and boy,

Here it is the question of freedom from guilt and the plea that children might be saved from the inevitable loss of innocence. This theological preoccupation is particularly noticeable in a poem like 'Spring and Fall' that deals with the doctrine of 'original sin'. Thomas on the other hand tells us very little about his religious convictions.

In Hopkins's last poems this spiritual struggle becomes more intense as he is plunged into despair by his own failures and impotence. He cannot understand why he, a priest and therefore one assumes a 'good man', should be so miserable when all around he sees 'sinners' ways prosper'. In a sense Hopkins is tortured by his religion and gets little real comfort from his faith.

By contrast Thomas's poems are alive with joy for life, even if most of his poems deal with the struggle of living from the land. He is concerned with real people and their problems. However bleak the situation he can usually find some redeeming factor that has made the character's life important. There is delight in man's triumph over the elements. 'Job Davies, eighty-five/ Winters old, and still alive' ('Lore') and, unlike Hopkins, even humour in 'Cynddylan on a Tractor':

> The clutch curses, but the gears obey
> His least bidding, and lo, he's
> Out of the farmyard, scattering hens
> Riding to work now as a great man should,[1]

The contrast between the two poets in the handling of their religious beliefs is the difference between Hopkins's intellectual approach and Thomas's Christian compassion. The distinction lies between a personal struggle for faith and a commitment to the essential goodness that Thomas sees around him. Although critics usually consider that Thomas is a dour and depressing poet in contrast to Hopkins, he is the one that is hopeful and celebrates the individual's small victories.[7]

WHAT'S SO GOOD ABOUT IT?

1 Good use of quotation.
2 Useful point about Roman Catholic doctrine.
3 Use of biographical knowledge.
4 Good use of specialized word.
5 Correct use of literary term.
6 Explains the contrast succinctly.
7 Succinct summary of the argument.

alliteration   repetition of a sound, especially at the beginnings of words; e.g. *Stone, bronze, stone, steel, stone* (Eliot).

allusion   a reference to another literary work, idea or historical event that enriches a poem by sharing the echoed material; e.g. the word *Fall* in Hopkins's 'Spring and Fall'.

couplet   a pair of lines

iambic pentameter   a metre of five units per line, each unit (technical term is a foot) consisting of an unstressed followed by a stressed component; e.g. *And all that mighty heart is lying still!* (Wordsworth).

image   a word picture used to make an idea come alive; e.g. a **metaphor**, **simile**, or **personification** (see separate entries).

irony/ironic   where the author or a character says the opposite of what he or she really thinks, or pretends ignorance, usually to ridicule an idea.

metaphor   a description of a thing as if it were something different but in some way similar; e.g. *The shining rafters/ Of that new world* (Thomas, 'Tramp').

narrative poem   a poem that tells a story.

parody   a line or passage that mimics another so as to make it look foolish or to attack it.

personification   a description of something as if it were a person; e.g. the stream in Hopkins's 'Inversnaid': *the fleece of his foam*.

quatrain   any four-lined stanza, rhymed or unrhymed.

rhyme   in 'pure rhyme' a matching of words with (1) a difference in the initial sound, followed by (2) a similarity with the vowel sound, and (3) with the end sound (king/sing/ring);

pure rhymes are called masculine when they have a strong ending (ban/can/man) and feminine when the ending is weaker (surly/curly/early).

rhyme scheme the pattern of rhymes in a stanza or poem, shown by using letters; e.g. an ABAB rhyme pattern indicates that the first and third lines rhyme and so do the second and fourth lines.

simile a comparison of two things, indicated by the words 'like' and 'as'; e.g. *Soft flesh ripening warm as corn* (Thomas, 'The Evacuee').

sonnet a poem of fourteen lines written in **iambic pentameter** (see p. 79); the first eight lines are called the *octave* and develop the proposition or matter of the poem; the next six lines (*sestet*) resolve or comment on the *octave*.

sprung-rhythm a complex rhythmical system, rediscovered and systematized by Hopkins, in which the important thing is the pattern of *stressed* syllables in a line, not how many syllables there are in the line all together.

stanza any group of one or more lines that is separate from any other group of lines.

stress the way words or parts of a word are emphasized when we speak. For example we tend to say re<u>qu</u>ire and <u>wa</u>ter.

symbol The use of a real object to explain complex ideas by its association with them; e.g. the Christian cross as a symbol of Christianity.

INDEX